PIZZA CZAR

ANTHONY FALCO

ABRAMS, NEW YORK

TABLE OF CONTENTS

FRESH MOZZARELLA

TOMATO SAUCE

PIZZA

ESTABLISHING THE BASELINE

NEAPOLITINISH PIZZA

WHITE PIES

PAN PIZZAS

FOREWORD

PHIL KRAJECK

It was April 2018, and Anthony and I had just finished working a long-ass day at my soon-to-open pizza restaurant, Folk, in Nashville. Anyone who has ever opened a restaurant knows that it's like giving birth, getting married, and getting divorced all at the same time. We came home, showered, and lit a fire in my backyard. We were exhausted. We needed a drink.

Anthony had traveled to Nashville to crash in my guest bedroom and help us figure out what the fuck we were doing. Sauce, dough, cheese—that was covered. It's the "How do we set ourselves up to execute consistently and quickly? How do we maintain the perfect oven floor temperature all service long? How do we get the ideal balance of extensibility and elasticity in our dough?"—that's the other part of Falco's genius that most people don't see. He's a consultant. You're in Sao Paolo and want to do grandma pie? You're in Mongolia and want to do Neapolitan? Call Falco. He'll arrive; dig into the supply chain; help you source the best dairy, flour, and tomatoes; and teach you how to properly use the oven you just spent thousands of dollars on. Falco knows the restaurant world and systems so well. Having him get on a plane—as a bro—and help me was invaluable.

Back to my backyard: After the aforementioned long-ass day, I opened a bottle of wine. And another. And another. At one point, Anthony looked deep into the fire and said, "We cook pizza with the stored energy of the sun."

Pizza Czar? How about Pizza Mystic?

See, the State of Pizza in Popular Culture over the past ten years is divided into two periods. B.F. and A.F.: Before Falco and After Falco. Anthony made pizza cool, mashing up art and culture and music and drugs and fucking delicious pizza and wine. That's why he's a legend. Because not only has he studied and tested his recipes a million times over, but he understands that pizza is a great unifier. It's joy and togetherness.

"I don't know how to do anything else," he's said to me, and likely countless people. Anthony Falco is a dude who just wants you to enjoy it as much as he does. Which is a lot. So much love, energy, and effort has gone into these recipes. Use them as a reference. And make so much pizza for your family and friends.

INTRODUCTION

I never meant to make my life about pizza. I also never asked to be called "Pizza Czar." But here I am, forty-one years old, and my life **revolves** around pizza. And now I'm writing a book **all about** pizza.
Mind. Officially. Blown.

Growing up I had a fierce love for pizza. But I imagined myself becoming a filmmaker, illustrator, or revolutionary (and I've done all three . . . in pizza). I was drawn to life in restaurants after realizing my artistic and revolutionary leanings would **not** be suited to office life.

I was raised in a household where my dad, a vegetarian (in Texas), denounced the factory farming he grew up around in Falls County. He was an outlaw, someone who thought cannabis and hemp should be legalized, took every psychedelic you could find in the '70s, and spent years in federal prison for smuggling hash. There was a lot of radical shit banging around the Falco house growing up, and food was foundational to it.

It had an effect. I found the **real** disruptors behind the bar, in the kitchen, and on the floor. Artists, writers, filmmakers, creatives—people who couldn't stomach the sacrifice of plugging into the nine-to-five. The cushy bubble of corporate stability felt like it could smother that flame. **These** were the people I wanted to surround myself with. But we needed gigs, so we found ourselves in the service industry.

Working in a restaurant, you develop comradery because you're on the battlefield together. You meet and work with new people from the world over. The work is physical. Everyone sweats and cleans together. And while there are rules, there is so much room for creativity.

I wouldn't even start making pizza until a decade into restaurant life, when I found myself at my first job in New York, where I'd been trying to move my entire life. And I wouldn't so much as come within **three feet** of the wood-fired oven for weeks after starting at Roberta's in Bushwick, Brooklyn. After I somehow got through my first shift topping pizzas without making a fool of myself, my boss said, "Falco, your pizza ninja training has begun."

Then he shoved a deck brush in my hand and said, "Now scrub the floors."

I was stoked. One of my favorite comics growing up was Usagi Yojimbo (which translates to "rabbit bodyguard") by Stan Sakai, the story of a samurai rabbit who, rather than join the prestigious martial arts school in town, trains with an angry old hermit living in the mountains. He carries water, splits wood, and cleans before becoming a rōnin (a masterless samurai). At this new gig, I'd become very good at splitting wood.

In 2010, I purchased a wood-fired mobile pizza oven with money I borrowed from my wife Rebecca's parents. I may have owned the pizza oven, but from that moment, it was pizza that owned me. That oven was more challenging and required more creativity than any restaurant I'd worked in. Cooking out in the elements in unfamiliar places and climates using different ingredients elevated my understanding of pizza. And by pizza, I mean dough. Dough is the hard part, the living part, what you obsess over if you commit to pizza as I did.

I came to oversee not just that oven but nine others and a team of pizza makers—probably 150 people between takeout, delivery, and frozen and mobile operations. My pizza masters called me the Pizza Czar. Back then, I felt this title may've been an attempt to keep me out of their traditional culinary hierarchy and make me sound silly. If my suspicion was correct, that backfired. Instead, the title sparks imaginations. (That, or it makes people think I sound like a pompous asshole.)

I made thousands of pizzas (some perfect, some failures), honed my skills, and was a part of a pizza program lauded as one of America's best. Then I sold my oven and said goodbye to my old life, and in the years since, I've traveled the globe making pizza, each challenge another chance to learn.

This book represents everything I've learned about making pizza over thirteen years: my mistakes (there've been plenty), my successes (luckily, I've had a few), and the recipes along the way.

As difficult as restaurant life is, in some ways it's a safe place. I mean, not **really**. It's a crazy place filled with dangers physical and emotional. But intellectually, after six months or so, you become familiar with the conditions and could probably work every station. Seasonal ingredients or menu refreshes add some variability, but the routine won't drastically differ. As a consultant, though, I've been thrown into situations making pizza in jungles and deserts, climates I've never encountered, hopping between hemispheres and among unfamiliar cultures. I've learned a lot about myself, about pizza making, and about dough—sometimes life-changing things. When I learned about natural fermentation it completely changed the way I approached dough and reshaped my understanding of the craft of pizza forever. The idea of employing the same technique that's been used to make bread rise for millennia—harvesting wild bacteria and yeast from the air, from us, from flour—there's something amazing, even revolutionary about it.

That is what I want to share.

In this book, I'll start by outlining the principles, tips, and methodologies I think every person needs to know when they embark on their pizza journey. Then I'll share recipes for you to try yourself. And, finally, in the back of the book, you'll find some pro moves to make your pizza dreams come true.

These pages contain a recipe collection developed over a lifetime of pizza, including favorites inspired by pies made at many of the restaurants I've helped open around the world. I'm proud of these recipes because they represent the challenge to come up with something unique over and over. I think you'll like them too.

THE ROAD TO PIZZA PRO

People ask, "How did you become a pizza czar?"

I didn't coin the term, but it's a good description of what I do: oversee pizza making the world over. People look to me to help manage their day-to-day, advise on recipes, logistics, and equipment, and problem-solve—whether that's finding employees or just needing to complain to someone about running a pizzeria.

Listen, a lot of people are faster, some are even better at making pizza, but as far as being an **expert** on making pizza? If a pizza czar is skilled in every area of running a pizzeria and many styles of pizza? That's me.

How'd I get here? It's an interesting journey. Well, hopefully.

HOW I GOT INTO COOKING

I started working as soon as it was legal for me to because my mom made me. She's a blue-collar liberal who grew up in inner-city Baltimore, one of the toughest people I know, and a hard worker with no time for slacking. I went to high school with rich kids who were getting summer internships at their dads' offices. *My* dad was on the run. But I thought I might be able to score a job in tech. When I told her as much she said, "Screw that, scrub toilets and help with the rent."

I was fifteen years old. I got a cashier job at a drugstore. Cleaning toilets was the best part. The job was monotonous, and I could set my watch to the frequency with which Jim Croce's "Operator" played. (I'm not anti-Croce, but in 1994, I was more of a Sonic Youth kinda guy.) I was relieved of my duties when a manager identified me (correctly) as a troublemaker.

My next job was front-of-house for Waterloo Ice House. Waterloo is the original name for Austin, Texas, where "ice house" is a term for places with cold beer and food. The Ice House (next to Waterloo Records, the legendary Austin record shop) served great nachos, I could pour draft beers (which, as a seventeen-year-old, was cool), they played great music, and I got to call names out over a microphone when orders were ready. One of the best jobs I've ever had.

I landed in Seattle in 1998 after couch surfing around the West Coast and Hawaii. I got a job as a dishwasher at a converted garage turned pool hall on Capitol Hill called . . . Garage. I'd get there in the morning and portion dough for rolls, cut and soak potatoes for fries, and clean squid for calamari. I was left mostly unsupervised. When dinner started all I had to do was crank out dishes. If I didn't cause problems with prep and I crushed it during the rush they'd make me something from the menu instead of giving me family meal, the usual meal served to staff. I was nineteen and I thought those cooks had it made: drinking, smoking, and making killer food.

After a while, I got a job as a pasta cook at a restaurant that today would be considered fast-casual. It was owned by an Italian guy and the pasta was pretty good, even with the name Pasta Ya Gotcha (I shit you not). I was an ambitious little shit mostly because the manager was a bad chef who was checked out. I felt like I could do a better job, and in the process, slide into that sweet manager pay raise of $7.50 an hour. And I did.

As cool as Pasta Ya Gotcha was, I've always been someone with a side hustle, and in my spare time I worked with friends doing web design. It was the late '90s and Flash was king. Somehow, through a combination of hard work, luck, and connections, we secured investment and I became a tech entrepreneur at the age of nineteen. I was making money instead of going to college and it seemed like a dream job, but then in June 2001 my nephew Frankie died in a car accident about a month before his fifth birthday. Frankie's father had been shot and killed two years earlier, and I had vowed to get rich in the tech business to support his son. Now, I

didn't want to do anything, and I didn't care about tech or getting rich, so I checked out. I ended up traveling around the world. It was a trip that had its ups and downs, including my first trips to Sicily and Thailand, among other places. In between my travels I was based out of Amsterdam, where I fell in love with the world's best French fries.

When my time in Amsterdam was winding down, a friend who had a space in a Seattle nightclub asked if I wanted to take it over and make it into whatever I wanted. I'd already developed a business plan for making the best *vlaamse frites* in America, so I took him up on it, and Frites was born. The business collected regional accolades during the three years I owned it, but ultimately, the lesson I took away was if you have an idea like this, you have to be prepared to do it forever. I wasn't prepared to peel potatoes forever.

I realized it was time to move to New York City.

ROBERTA'S

I started as a part-time pizza cook at a restaurant called Roberta's in Bushwick that had just opened in 2008. I'd been bartending with the people who would become the founders of Roberta's, and I was making decent money, but it wasn't something I wanted to do forever. I had *no idea* what I wanted to do forever. I was in my late twenties and nothing had stuck. So when they told me about their new restaurant, I figured . . . learn pizza? Why not?

I've always loved pizza. I mean, *loved* it. It's one thing to cook things you like, but to cook something you *love* and be able to make it for yourself and your friends? That's awesome. I liked being able to cook a pizza *exactly* how I wanted it: the ideal amounts of cheese, toppings, and sauce. The ability to get your own perfect pizza without an intermediary is . . . magical.

Learning how to operate a wood-fired oven got under my skin. I couldn't get enough. You can learn how to use a wood-fired oven in one day—picking a pizza up, putting it in, pulling it out—but you can spend *a lifetime* learning to manage fire and operate an oven. Everything from building a fire (a great meditative exercise) to learning how to push the oven to its limit hooked me. Hanging out at the bar with friends after, I'd smell like a cross between a fresh-baked pizza and a campfire. It was awesome.

I started the winter Roberta's opened. There was no heat, and business was slow. Bushwick was just starting to become super-hip and Roberta's was *not* on anyone's radar. This was pre-Instagram, and it took awhile for a new restaurant to be discovered. There was time for experimentation, and a few people

Tossing Pizza

The first guys I remember throwing pizza in the air at Roberta's were the Ojai guys—Ben Wiseman and Irfan Zaidi—surfer dudes from Ojai, California. The way they made pizza was laid-back and smooth as hell. It wasn't until I started working on Roberta's takeout and delivery project that I watched them and was like, "I gotta learn how to do this." Now I throw pizza because it's fun. But if you even out the crust and start tossing, it makes the shape pleasing. The centrifugal force stretches the dough out evenly.

who taught me a lot about pizza were there all the time.

It was Anjali Suneja who taught me how to open up dough. To this day, I use her terminology. Picture it: We're in this garage in Bushwick off the Morgan L stop in an area that's mostly industrial warehouses. Anjali says, "Look at this beautiful dough ball. It's spent twenty-four hours becoming round. It wants to be round. Let's let it be round." It was a hippie-dippie approach, but I was raised by hippies, so it was a language I understood. It was just the two of us making pizza in the early days. Her positive energy was great.

The other person who influenced me was Mauro Soggiu. Mauro was one of the original guys, and he's from Italy. Mauro had . . . maybe not the most positive teaching approach. He'd quickly call out anything that didn't meet his standards. His famous line was, "This pizza, to me, is a shit." I still think that's hilarious and remember it every time I make a shitty pizza.

But Mauro was a great teacher when it came to the oven. The original oven came from someone he knew in Northern Italy, so he and it were connected. He also knew a lot of interesting topping combinations and had a base of traditional Italian cooking knowledge. I've worked for lots of people well-versed in Italian cuisine since, but not like Mauro. As many Italians are, he's more passionate about food than most people on earth, with *strong* opinions about pizza toppings. He had a pizza topping for every seasonal situation you could throw at him.

Once, it was prosciutto e funghi, *prosciutto cotto* (which is cooked, not salt-cured) and dried porcinis with cream added to the tomato sauce. That's funny because depending on the Italian you talk to, you'll hear "Never put cream on pizza!" or "Always put cream on pizza." There are as many rules in Italian cooking as Italians to break those same rules.

This was great. The family I knew growing up was my dad's, all Sicilian-Americans, generations removed. There were a few old-timers who'd come *from* Sicily but I hadn't spent the time I craved in an Italian community. Learning about Italy's different regional cuisines beyond Sicilian made going to work exciting. Soon I became skilled enough to make pizza start to finish.

In those early days, Roberta's felt like a clubhouse. Mauro and I would be in the front making pizza, maybe even while drinking wine, and he'd rush to the dining room to mingle with anyone he knew who came in. And while sometimes the best thing you can do when you run a restaurant is work the room, this left me alone in the kitchen. He knew I could handle the oven.

One day I complained about my frustrations—inconsistency in the dough I was given, confusion over the pecking order—to one of the partners I used to bartend with. "Sounds like you need to step up and be the man," he said. "If you want to step up and be the man, then you're the man."

That was my sign to take the reins, which was tough because suddenly I was corralling people who used to tell me what to do. The dough guy quit, and this ended up being a turning point both at Roberta's and for my pizza making. Until that point, someone had always made dough for me. Suddenly I was working eighteen-hour days, making dough, doing dinner prep, working the oven during service, and then starting dough for the next day until four in the morning.

Anyone who makes pizza will tell you how many variables there are when it comes to dough from one day to the next. "It's the weather! It's the flour! It's, it's, it's!" That makes regimentation important.

I had what I then called a dough recipe, but I now understand it wasn't a recipe at all. It was just the weight of flour, water, and salt. There were no mixing times or proofing temperatures. It was three numbers written on a paper scrap. This is where I started to understand that methodologies can be more important than recipes.

So I had an approach to dough, but I needed someone methodical, who wanted to be there, to help make it. Margarito was a Roberta's dishwasher who wanted to be more than that. That's always the best candidate.

With Margarito helping on dough duty, it immediately became more consistent. He became Roberta's backbone. You could count on that dough. That's the hardest thing: not just making something great but making it consistently. With the dough handled, we were able to explore toppings, topping combinations, and ingredients. We could make seasonal pizzas and step up to the attention we started getting.

I made other changes in those early days. Inspired by accounts I read online about former software engineer turned viral pizza recipe creator and restaurateur Jeff Varasano, I developed a sourdough starter instead of using commercial yeast. I also changed cook times. Some folks on the team liked to cook pizza at a lower temperature so it was lightly colored without black spots. Others preferred cooking hotter for a Neapolitan look. I loved the way the pizza looked when you cooked it fast at a high temperature, so *that's* the approach I put in place.

This proved fortunate. As we were written about and Bushwick became increasingly popular, we got busier. We wouldn't have survived if we were waiting on pizzas to cook at lower temperatures. As the restaurant got busier, we needed to cook pizzas faster.

And after the *New York Times* visited in 2008 and again in 2011 to review Roberta's, it was never slow again.

Years later, as a pizza consultant, I would draw on these development experiences and compress them into a week of on-site training with my client. I come in, and *boom*—we establish a base: the dough. And once we settle on a dough they love, we create a system so they can recreate it every day. It's only once you have the base that you can talk about a signature pizza and create a menu.

I spent almost nine years at Roberta's. I was able to focus on different flavor combinations and seasonal pizzas, and experiment with incorporating every meat, vegetable, and seafood ingredient you can imagine. You name it, we tried it. That's how I became a pizza pro—fucking up a lot—me and Margarito, Mauro, Anjali, and the other great people who came through those doors.

Goodbye, Roberta's. Hello, World.

It would be nice to say I had a grand vision to become an international pizza consultant. That's not what happened. I was fired and I had no idea what to do next. I made an Instagram post that thanked everyone I'd worked with and learned from and I got a huge response from that. I signed a contract in Brazil for a place that would become Bráz Elettrica and changed my bio to "International Pizza Consultant." It had a nice ring to it. Since then, I've made pizza across America and all around the world.

INTERNATIONAL CONSULTING:
PHILOSOPHY

What Is Pizza?

In short, pizza is wheat, tomato, and cheese. I'll get to those three pillars, but let's start by defining terms and discussing styles.

Pizza can be anything you want, but words should have meaning, so I like to narrow the scope. In this book, pizza will always be a leavened dough, and I encourage folks toward **natural leavening**. More on that in "Natural Fermentation, What the Hell Is That?" on page 249.

We'll stretch that naturally leavened dough into a circle, a square, or a rectangle. Often we'll top it with tomato and cheese. Some pizzas will not have either, but those are the exceptions. The dough-sauce-cheese paradigm is our baseline.

THOUGHTS ON PIZZA STYLES

There are two styles in this book: pizza cooked on a stone and pizza cooked in a pan. Some will say, "Grandma pizza is this many inches tall," or "Detroit-style pizza must be made in *this* pan." To them I say: It's personal preference. There's no Official Pizza Governing Body. But mostly pizza is round with a raised crust and a flat area covered with toppings—tomato sauce and cheese. *That's* pizza.

There's a cottage industry of experts forever trying to categorize every pizza style. They'll debate Neapolitan versus Neo-Neapolitan or whether midwestern, party-cut pizzas can be called "bar pies" for hours. You can try to regiment styles and regional specialties. I won't. I'm taking a big picture look.

Want to take my grandma recipe and cook it in a Detroit pan? Go ahead. Will it be Detroit-style pizza? I don't know. Are you in Detroit? Like, where do these things come from? **Be free, with words and with pizza**. We have to classify things to an extent, but in general, keep it simple.

Most pizzas cooked on the oven floor are round. Most pan pizzas are square. As always, there are exceptions. Round pan pizzas are great too.

Zoom out. Take a global perspective of the pizza scene circa 1943. There are pockets of wood-fired pizzerias in Italy (mostly in Naples and Rome) and others serving Italian immigrant communities in Buenos Aires and São Paulo and on America's East Coast. These were round pies, on the higher hydration side, stretched thin, and minimally topped with tomatoes, cheese, veggies, and occasionally meat or seafood.

I've spent thirteen years working almost exclusively within this style of pizza. I think about it, eat it, live it, breathe it, research it, read about it, and talk about it every day. Know what? I don't know what to label it. To me, it's pizza. Wet dough, slow fermentation, hand stretching, simple toppings, and high-temperature cooking on the oven floor.

After the '40s, something interesting happened to pizza, Italian food, and Italians in general. Italians went from one of America's most vilified immigrant groups to being celebrated. Musicians, actors, directors, athletes, and artists all helped Italian-American communities—and their food—become popular.

Pizza was in demand. If there weren't Italian enclaves to serve the demand, non-Italians stepped up to fill it. Pizza started changing. Either unable or unwilling to study traditional techniques, these newcomers created new styles, including dry doughs, quick fermentation, doughs that were stretched through a roller or spread and cooked on screens in conveyor ovens, and an increase in topping amount and variety. These nontraditional pizza styles conquered America and then the world.

Of the world's top ten pizza chains, only Sbarro has real Italian roots. This matters, because in this book, we aren't making crackers and we won't use screens. We will push traditional techniques and ingredients. Sure, I will break rules and piss purists off, but the pizzas in this book are rooted in traditions of the Italian diaspora.

Fermentation's Effect on Dough Shape

Under-fermented dough is a lot easier to make round, but it's not going to be as delicious. A well-fermented dough won't necessarily be easy to make round, but it will taste great.

BIG PIZZA AND PIZZA IN THE DIASPORA

I do see a division in styles with a historical connection to the global Italian and Sicilian diaspora, and the ones that were made up once the demand for pizza outstripped the supply of Italians available to make it.

Consider Pizza Hut, the world's second-largest pizza chain. It was started by brothers Dan and Frank Carney. One was writing a thesis on collective bargaining. ("They wouldn't let me write on franchising," Dan said, explaining the idea was too new to professors in the '50s.) They wanted to establish a proof of concept, so they picked pizza because it was trendy, borrowed $600 to start the first location, and then looked for a recipe.

The Carneys found a guy named John Bender, who worked at a pizzeria in Bloomington, Indiana. According to pizza blog Passion-4-Pizza, Bender remembered the sauce recipe but forgot how to make dough, so they looked up a recipe for French bread. The Carneys went for it, and their gamble paid off in 1977 when they sold to PepsiCo for $320 million.

Meanwhile, for fifty years before the Carneys disrupted the world by franchising their radical pizzas, there were large Italian communities on America's East Coast and in Brazil and Argentina making and eating pizza, mostly for their communities.

Italians were some of the first Europeans to come to the Americas. Their numbers were small until 1870. With the formation of the Republic of Italy in 1861 came the collapse of feudalism and other factors that led to the largest wave of human migration in history. From 1890 to 1914, some twelve million mostly agrarian Italians from the south and Sicily took ships to the Americas. Most went to Brazil and Argentina, but the United States took millions, many clustered in New York, New Jersey, and Connecticut.

It's funny–in São Paulo, its oldest pizzeria, Castelões Cantina & Pizzaria (established 1924), has more in common with Frank Pepe in Connecticut (founded 1925) than with most other pizzerias in Brazil or America. Its look, the service style–both have neon-mounted signs indoors and white tile ovens. Sure, Castelões is wood-fired and Pepe uses coal, but both are cooked close to the same high heat that results in similarly beautifully charred crusts.

Sicilian pizza is an American thing. In Sicily, the roots of "Sicilian" pizza, they wouldn't consider that pizza. They think of pizza as from Naples. And in Naples, *nothing* square is *pizza*.

See, there's a problem with naming Italian foods. Italy as a nation was a project that didn't begin until 1861 when the peninsula and the islands of Sicily and Sardinia were united under the House of Savoy. Italy was a country in name, with variations in language, customs, and food.

The roots of the Sicilian pizza *Americans* know are found all over Italy: focaccia. Purists today would call Sicilian pizza a type of focaccia. Sicily's version reflected the island's products: sea salt, oregano, anchovies, olive oil, and sheep's milk cheese. When tomatoes were introduced, Sicilian bakeries incorporated the New World import into focaccia, and *sfinciuni*, a bread with a tall, airy crumb, was born.

The tomatoes were combined with breadcrumbs, olive oil, onion, anchovy, and sometimes caciocavallo (a Southern-Italian, teardrop-shaped, stretched-curd cheese made with sheep's or cow's milk) or Pecorino (sheep's milk cheese). It was a tomato pie—a side or on-the-go snack.

As Sicilians immigrated with other Italians, they found themselves and their foods in contact. Although the first pizzerias in the Americas were started by immigrants from Campania, soon Sicilians, Calabrese, Barese, and others influenced the pizza world.

I grew up eating square pizzas my great-grandmother made. She never called them "pizza." They were *faccia di vecchia*. They were grandma pizza in a sense because she was a grandma, but did they follow the "rules" of grandma pizza? Doubtful. A few pizzerias are credited with inventing "grandma pizza." They're awesome—but I call bullshit. Grandmas have made square pies for centuries; how can you *invent* grandma pizza? Popularize it? Maybe. Lots of stuff around pizza is marketing and writers who coin terminology. Nothing wrong with it. You just can't get too worked up.

Making consistently round pizza is harder than it seems. Does pizza have to be round? Honestly, I don't care if it's oblong or amoeba-shaped (beginners will make amoeba pizzas). Does it taste amazing? That's the point. But things are different in a pizzeria or when you're training someone to make hundreds of pizzas a day. A randomly shaped pizza could taste great, but those pizzas won't taste the same one day to the next.

For example, sauce amount won't be consistent. If you're using a portion spoon to sauce your pizza (let's say 2 ounces/60 ml of sauce on a 12-inch/30-cm pizza), depending on the oven and other toppings, that could be the perfect amount, but what will happen when you stretch it out to a 14-inch (36-cm) surfboard-looking thing? If you fill the area inside the crust with that amount of sauce, it will end up dry, and if it gets squished on its way into the oven and is only 10 inches (25 cm) wide, it will be overly saucy.

If you let a cook send out not-very-round pizzas, the shapes will be a free-for-all. I won't say it's easy to make round pizza over and over, and these recipes won't make it easier. They're delicious—wet and sticky—not easy. But it's possible to get good at making round pies, and I'll teach you how to master the technique.

You may be thinking, "There must be an easier way to make consistently round pizza." There is. Chains use pizza screens, round mesh (picture a screen door) you can stretch dough out on and put into the oven (instead of launching dough off a peel), an innovation from pizza going mainstream. Owners were financially motivated and had no hang-ups about tradition.

None of the century-old Italian-owned pizzerias that remain from the original wave of immigrants use screens or conveyor ovens. It's not like they don't know that they exist, it's because, right or wrong, they're bound by tradition. Nobody wants to be the first pizza maker in four generations to use them just because it's easier.

Taste is subjective, but I think the majority of pizza lovers would prefer a pizza cooked on the surface of a brick oven. My career as a pizza maker and these recipes are about aspiring to make the best pizza. To strive for greatness. That isn't often the easiest way.

THE THREE PILLARS OF PIZZA:

WHEAT, TOMATOES, AND CHEESE

Now that the philosophical stuff is out of the way, let's talk about wheat, tomatoes, and cheese and what they mean for pizza.

WHEAT

As you know, wheat is a grass. Over millennia it was bred to produce larger wheat berries. It was a crucial food for humanity's transition from hunter-gathering to agricultural society. The harvesting of einkorn (wild wheat) predates agriculture and was so abundant in places like Göbekli Tepe (the world's most ancient temple structures) in modern-day southeastern Turkey that humans were able to build megalithic structures in permanent settlements by harvesting this natural resource.

In the West, wheat and agrarian civilization are inextricably linked. Bread that would be recognizable to us was a part of life to the average Egyptian, Mesopotamian, Greek, or Roman. Beehive-shaped wood ovens almost identical to our wood-burning pizza ovens have been found all over the ancient Roman world.

Surely, they made some kind of flatbread topped with herbs and fats. But per our definition, we can't call those pizzas. They lacked tomatoes and mozzarella.

Before getting too specific, let's talk big picture on how to choose a flour. Listen, I'm not a scientist, but I appreciate the scientific method. I learned everything from trial and error, and I get the best information when I'm measuring everything. It's important because I'm constantly experimenting with flours in places around the world I'm visiting for the first time.

Potassium Bromate: Just Say No

I always want to use flour that has *not* been chemically bleached or bromated.

All flour will begin bleaching naturally as it's milled and exposed to oxygen in the air. But it takes time to naturally age and bleach flour, so a few chemicals, including potassium bromate, were patented to accelerate the process. Potassium bromate is a flour "improver" that strengthens dough, but has also been classified as a class 2B carcinogen by the International Agency for Research on Cancer. It's banned as a flour additive in many countries. California requires warning labels on bromated flour, but unfortunately, it's widespread on America's East Coast.

Why don't I use it? It's unnecessary.

Flour is milled wheat. That's all it needs to be. But it's often not that simple. When milling became centralized and mass-produced, flour's shelf life needed extending. By eliminating most of the bran and the germ with the use of roller mills, you get a soft, white flour with a longer shelf life. The bran and germ can cause rancidity but contribute nutrition. The manufacturers' solution? Enrich flour with vitamins and minerals, then bleach with chemicals to make it indestructible.

It's not quite as good as the real thing. It's important to understand that flour doesn't last forever. So if you choose a local stone-milled high-extraction flour (a high level of bran and germ, and thus high levels of minerals), remember its shorter shelf life.

Bottom line? No chemicals, please. In addition, choose freshly milled, naturally nutritious flour, instead of processed and enriched flour if possible.

Play with as many flours as you can, then blend them to create something that speaks to you. Sometimes a blend can be better than the sum of its parts. For more information on choosing your flours, see the "Products" section on page 242.

ꝒDough Extensibility and Elasticity

Think about extensibility as when you lift and stretch dough. If it stays stretched and doesn't snap back, it's extensible. You get extensibility from the type of wheat, hydration, mixing, and shaping. Elastic is the opposite: When you stretch dough and it snaps to its original shape and you have to keep stretching. You want balance. You don't want dough falling apart when you're opening it. My doughs are on the extensible side.

TOMATO

Solanum lycopersicum

XITOMATL

The wild tomato is native to the Andean mountain range and most likely cultivated by early Meso-American civilizations. The word comes from the later Aztecs, who continued cultivating *tomatl* ("plump fruit" in the Nahuatl language) and the Spanish who brought them to Europe and called them *tomate*.

By all accounts, tomatoes were not an immediate sensation. They had a short growing season and weren't very nutritious. Europeans, and especially Italians, viewed food differently than we do today. They were influenced by the humoral theories of Galen and Hippocrates systematized in ancient Greece— the body's four humors (blood, phlegm, black bile, and yellow bile) were associated with the elements and had to be balanced for healthy body and mind. Tomatoes were thought to influence black bile. Not very appetizing sounding. By the seventeenth century, Europeans started seeing food and digestion from a more mechanical and chemical point of view, and tomatoes grew in prevalence.

The first tomato recipe appears in print in *The Modern Steward, or The Art of Preparing Banquets Well*, a cookbook published in the 1690s in Naples by Antonio Latini, a steward to a cardinal-nephew of then-pope Urban VIII. Latini sounds like a guy running a big staff in a castle who was like, "Man, we gotta write this shit down, people make stuff different every time and I'm getting in trouble."

It's about this time we can assume the first recognizable pizza was made. But it wasn't until the late eighteenth century that the plum-shaped tomato became widespread in Europe. The tomato, originally small, round, and golden, was brought from the Americas to Europe by the Spanish and it was the Neapolitans that bred it into the red, plum-shaped tomato that would come to be known as the San Marzano.

We'll make several tomato-based pizza sauces, but mostly we will use canned tomatoes seasoned with salt and olive oil, uncooked.

CHEESE

mozzarella

milkfat globule

casein matrix

MILK

Let's be real: It's the combination of mozzarella and tomato on dough that makes pizza, pizza.

Fresh Mozzarella: In Italy it's fresh, usually made from the milk of semi-wild water buffalo, and it's typically amazing. In America, I don't use lots of buffalo mozzarella. We have a lot of great cow's milk mozzarella (called *fior di latte* in Italy) and good producers to choose from. You can get fresh product fairly easily, especially on the East Coast and other areas with active artisanal food communities.

Low-Moisture or Aged Mozz: America's most widely consumed pizza cheese. It's what you'll find on New York–style pizza, commercial pizza, even New Haven pizza. The main differences are, after it's made, it's pressed into blocks to remove moisture, and aged.

Fresh mozzarella is supposed to be made and eaten the same day. In Italy, buffalo mozzarella is made in the morning, put in Styrofoam containers, and sent via Vespa to pizzerias. *Ciao, bella!* What isn't eaten on pizzas is tossed or used another way that day. The reality is, Italy has just as much of an industrial food system as the United States, but this is the ideal way that mozzarella should be consumed and used.

In America, there's an interesting phenomenon with fresh mozzarella. Milk producers make curd, package it unsalted, and ship it to delis and pizzerias, where people stretch *their own* mozzarella in the morning. It's awesome. We'll get into that.

Fresh mozzarella is great for Neapolitanish-style pizza, high-temp cooking, home ovens, and New York–style gas deck ovens, but it runs the risk of breaking, over-melting, and making a wet mess. It also doesn't have the nostalgia factor for Americans. Aged and low-moisture mozzarella are great for what Americans generally think of as pizza; it performs better at lower temperatures. But good fresh mozzarella is crucial to making pizza at home.

What do I look for? Many are under-salted. Stretching mozzarella from curd, which I like to do when I can, allows control over seasoning. That's not a problem with low-moisture mozzarella, which runs salty. You also have whole milk and part-skim aged or low-moisture mozz. Sometimes people use a combination of low-moisture and whole milk mozzarellas to get that New York–style slice consistency.

Later in this book, I will briefly cover making your own mozzarella with two methods. You'll find those recipes beginning on page 40.

"When Should I Use Low-Moisture Mozz by Itself?"

When you're doing New York–style or thin-crust pizza. It's nostalgic. You can also use a mix of fresh mozzarella with low-moisture mozz. That's delicious. Just don't use too much—things get wet and greasy.

SHREDDING

FRESH MOZZARELLA

What size? You want to start with a whole ball and tear off chunks. Start with bigger chunks. How big? The size of a medium coin, like a US nickel or quarter. If you're making your own mozz for these recipes, don't worry too much about what size of a ball to form.

PRE-SHREDDED CHEESE

Always shred your own. Most pre-shredded mozzarella is coated with anti-caking agents. Worst-case scenario? They're chemical. Best case? They're cellulose–basically derived from wood pulp. You don't know how much caking agent was used, and it can inhibit the way mozzarella melts and stretches.

SHRED SIZE

If you do thin shreds, the cheese runs the risk of over-melting. New York-style pizzerias usually use a shredder with half-inch holes to create thick shreds. Why? So that even after spending a long time in the oven at lower temperatures, it doesn't melt into a puddle of grease. You want your cheese to melt fully and brown a bit. You don't want it to break.

HOW FAR AHEAD DO I SHRED?

Don't prep anything too far in advance. You can try shredding the day before but it can clump, especially if it's at room temp but even in the fridge. As with the rest of your ingredients besides the dough, shred as close to the topping time as possible. Think, max 48 hours.

TOOLS OF THE TRADE

WHETHER YOU'RE A FIRST-TIMER OR OLD HAND, IF YOU'RE EXCITED ABOUT PIZZA, I WANT YOU TO ENJOY MAKING ANY OR EVERY PIZZA IN THIS COOKBOOK. YOU MAY ALREADY HAVE THE TOOLS TO DO SO, BUT IF NOT, HERE ARE MY FAVORITES BASED ON YEARS OF TRYING COUNTLESS MANUFACTURERS (AND SOME TIPS).

CAST-IRON PAN

It's great for pizza—a slow heat conductor that, if warmed slowly, distributes the heat evenly and creates a beautiful, uniformly cooked crust. I like Lodge (made in America, baby).

STEEL FRYING PAN

I bought a set of All-Clad Cookware in 2000 with the first paycheck from my first business, Shock Fusion, a Flash web design company my friend Philip and I started in 1999 that got funding in the dot-com boom. I still use that cookware twenty years later. A steel frying pan is indestructible and it's just below cast iron in terms of slow, even heat distribution.

WOODEN PIZZA PEEL

A good wood pizza peel is a classic tool. For millennia, a wooden paddle with a handle was the only way bread got into an oven. Even today this is the go-to for pizza. You'll build pizzas on a wooden peel then slide them onto your stone.

METAL PIZZA PEEL

A wooden peel is great for building pizza and launching it, but a metal peel is ideal for *moving* pizzas around while they cook. The thin metal can slip under the pizza and won't burn. You can use it to spin the pizza in the oven so it heats evenly and then to pull it out. You can also use it to pick up the pizza from a floured surface. It can take time to master, but if your pizza is properly floured, you can scoop it up quickly without messing up the shape.

Treat Your Wooden Peel Right

Treat your peel with John Boos Mystery Oil after every use. Just rub the oil on and then remove it with a scraper. Over time it will seal and waterproof it. You don't ever want to wash a wooden peel with water at first. After a long time of treating it with Mystery Oil, you might be able to wash it. But you shouldn't need to. The oil will keep it clean.

DIGITAL SCALE

Not an optional purchase. Do you need a scale to make great pizza? No. Nonnas the world over crank out amazing pizzas, pastas, and all kinds of mamma mia food without measuring a damn thing. But if you're reading this, I'm betting you're *not* anyone's nonna. So buy a scale and use it to measure every single thing. It's *not* hard, it will advance your knowledge, you'll get better faster, and you'll come to appreciate consistency.

When I travel to make pizza, this is one of the only tools I bring. By measuring and using percentages in recipes, you can adjust so you aren't shooting in the dark. For home cooks, I recommend a gram scale with an accuracy of 0.01 gram. You want this for smaller batches of dough and things like salt and yeast. A minimum 5-kilo scale with an accuracy of 1 gram— generally for anything weighing more than 500 grams—is also recommended.

MIXING BOWLS

I hand-mix most of my smaller dough batches in a large mixing bowl. If I'm honest it's because I don't want to pull my mixer out from underneath the counter. I like to have three steel mixing bowls (13-quart, 5-quart, and 3-quart). I use the 13-quart for my flours; the 5-quart for water, starter, and oil; and the 3-quart for salt. I have multiples of these three sizes.

DOUGH SCRAPER/ CUTTER

A plastic bowl scraper is a great tool for cleaning mixers and removing dough from a bowl. It's a flat rectangular-shaped piece of hard plastic with one curved side so it can scrape the bowl clean. A dough knife or dough cutter is a thin piece of rectangular metal with a wooden or plastic handle on one end. It's for portioning dough.

BAKING STEEL/STONE

The heat from a stone can be softer and even, whereas a steel can be harsh. Whichever you use, it's important to have *two* layers of steel or stone. One level where you cook the pizza and another above radiating heat *downward*.

IMMERSION BLENDER

An essential tool and the best way to make sauce. A stand-up blender adds too much oxygen and turns tomatoes orange. And most blenders are hard to clean and require space. An immersion blender can be used for other sauces and whipping eggs and cream. Food mills are great, but they're time-consuming to use and you'll never get the same smooth texture.

FOOD PROCESSOR

A food processor is nice to have and can save you time. If you don't have one, you can do almost everything in this book you'd use one for with a mortar and pestle.

CHEESE GRATER

A good box grater allows you to produce cheeses grated at different sizes and shapes. The largest size will help your mozzarella from over-melting. The fine-tooth grate will result in powdery Parmigiano that dissolves into sauce.

MICROPLANE

Great for zesting citrus and grating cheese for finishing pizzas (Parmigiano and Pecorino).

PIZZA PANS

A good pizza pan is a great place for an amateur pizza maker to start or an advanced one to geek out. The amateur can make pizza without worrying about stretching and launching the pizza. The advanced pizza maker gets to explore the finer points of crumb structure. I love the pans from LloydPans. They have traditional Sicilian, Detroit, and round pans in all shapes and sizes. LloydPans also makes aluminum lids (optional) that allow you to proof and stack pans.

PLASTIC WRAP

Good plastic wrap is important to utilize the sheet pan technique of dough proofing. Proofing boxes are expensive and bulky, they hide the fermentation process, and they trap air inside, making for less nimble proofing and retarding. A simple, cheap, and stackable sheet pan with a layer of plastic wrap covering the dough balls is my preference.

COMMON U.S. BAKING SHEET DIMENSIONS

Conventional Size Name	Outer Width (in)	Outer Depth (in)	Outer Height (in)
FULL	26	18	1
TWO-THIRDS/ THREE-QUARTERS	21	15	1
HALF	18	13	1
QUARTER	13	9.5	1
EIGHTH	6.5	9.5	1

SHEET PANS (AKA SHEET TRAYS OR BUN PANS)

A standardized group of baking sheets. A full sheet is 18 by 26 inches (46 by 66 cm). They're also available in two-thirds, half, quarter, and eighths, and are made with fiberglass, aluminum, steel, and coated metals. For proofing I prefer fiberglass. Aluminum oxidizes and transfers flecks. Steel is great for roasting and proofing but heavy and pricier. I can fit a half sheet in my home fridge. There are also sheet pan lids, which allow stacking. In this book, when I refer to a sheet tray, it's an 18-by-13-inch (46-by-33-cm) half sheet pan. While you can cook the pan pizzas in these, the fact that they aren't nonstick and they're thinner means the results won't be as good as with a proper pizza pan.

PIZZA TINS

You'll need metal tins to transfer pizzas to when they come out of the oven, and you can serve your pizza on these as well. (Peel, tin, cutter—your basic setup.)

LADLES

Flat-bottom ladles allow you to dole out the same amount of sauce every time and the flat bottom allows even spreading. I like a 1-ounce (30-ml) and 2-ounce (60-ml) ladle for home pizza making.

A NOTE ON OVENS

A full breakdown on the different types of pizza ovens can be found on page 258. If you, like many home cooks, are starting out with just the regular oven in your kitchen, you'll want to consult the "Home Ovens" section on page 264.

Thin & Crispy Pizzas

I started making my Thin & Crispy dough after a client told me their favorite style was New Jersey thin and crispy bar-style pizza and they hired me to recreate it. The partners behind Uptown Social—Keith Benjamin, Kara Graves, and Jonathan Arzt—wanted to open something in that style in Charleston, South Carolina. Specifically, they sent me to Star Tavern in Orange, New Jersey, an hour's drive west of Manhattan (Keith grew up going there). I loved the vibe. Star Tavern has been owned and operated by the Vayianos family since 1980. It has classic wooden booths, a long bar with old-school beer signs above it, and even some arcade games.

The kitchen was open, so I saw their process. Dough was rolled out with a roller in a pile of flour, then placed on a customized pan that had half of the lip cut off, topped, and put into a deck oven. Halfway through the cook, pies were slid directly onto the deck to be finished. They were very thin and crispy with a healthy layer of cheese and sauce.

If I lived around the corner I'd get a booth with my kids frequently, but I didn't want my thin and crispy pizza to be a cracker crust. I want even my thin, bar-style pizza to have a crumb, like bread. I worked through various flours and blends developing a crispier pizza with enough strength to be thin. I went with a blend of high-protein and all-purpose flours.

The breakthrough was when I brought fat levels way up.

Olive oil and other fats are *not* allowed in Vera Pizza Napoletana (VPN) pizza making (neither is sugar), but depending on who you talk to it seems many pizzerias in Naples *do* use lard or olive oil. Fat in dough in small amounts makes the crumb more tender and in large amounts makes pizza crispier. In the past, I'd only used up to 3%, but for Thin & Crispy (Pizza Hut trademarked Thin N' Crispy), I decided to see what would happen when you go *way* up. At 8 to 10% olive oil, the outside of the crust fries a little, while the crumb stays tender.

Most everyone agrees higher fat in doughs makes the crumb more tender, so the debate is the effect on the crust exterior. The prevailing idea is to lower the hydration with no or little fat, producing a cracker-like crust. I tried this and didn't like the flavor, crumb structure, or anything besides the crispiness—it was dry. So I moved in the other direction, to high hydration (a 60 to 70% range) and high oil (8 to 10%). That may seem counterintuitive, but it worked. It makes a crispy, delicious pizza.

METHODOLOGIES

Having a clearly defined recipe and methodology is vital for successful, delicious, and repeatable pizza. I'll use basic baker's percentages for dough recipes and step-by-step instructions for my methodologies.

Baker's percentages are a simple way of writing and communicating a pizza recipe. It assumes you're using flour and that flour percentage will always be 100%. All other ingredients will be measured by weight, **as a percentage of the flour weight**. In this book, baker's percentages will be used in their most basic form.

Dough will differ batch to batch, day to day. There are many factors—you're dealing with living microorganisms and, usually, a changing environment. To mitigate that flux in some way, weighing everything is vital. It makes things as simple and accurate as possible. I always weigh **all** ingredients and write things down in baker's math.

The water in your baker's percentage is your hydration rate. It's a way of understanding dough and communicating recipes. So, when I'm testing a pizza I'm feeling the dough and baking it, thinking about how I can adjust hydration up or down as a percentage. And if I'm talking to another pizza maker and I ask what the hydration is, the answer as a percentage will tell me more than the amount of water in any given batch size or recipe. Using baker's percentages also allows you to scale recipes easily because if you are making dough with the same percentages, it doesn't matter if you're making fifteen or fifteen hundred dough balls.

Salts by Weight

Because of their crystalline structure, salts have different weights by volume. That's why it's important to weigh *all* ingredients for recipes, but *especially* important to weigh salt. The salt should be a specific percentage of the weight of the thing you're cooking.

WEIGHING INGREDIENTS

I've learned this the hard way: Every recipe should start with weighing ingredients. That's the foundation of my methodology. I adjust based on environment and desired results. Whether I'm teaching a client or a home cook, I create systems that encourage consistency.

Start by weighing all dry ingredients (salt and any flours) in separate bowls. I weigh different flours in separate containers in case something goes wrong with the scale. I almost always use a blend of flours. I note total flour weight in the baker's percentage recipe and how flours are divided in the margins. Wets should also be weighed separately. Then in two large bowls, mix the dry ingredients in one bowl and the wets in the other. If you're using a mixer, put the wets in first, then the drys.

SALT

You *must* avoid iodized table salt. I don't like the idea of 2% anti-caking agents or sodium iodine, and it's too punchy taste-wise, especially at 3% of flour. Do *not* use it. Kosher salt is fine. It isn't iodized, so it won't ruin dough's flavor (some say its coarseness prevents it from blending well, but I've never noticed that). Sea salt can be affordable, is usually additive-free, and trace minerals may improve taste. Go with the least processed choice: sea salt.

Fine Sicilian sea salt is fantastic, and it's been made the same way forever on the western side of Sicily, centered around shallow pools between the coastal towns of Marsala and Trapani. The area is protected, so it's clean. As sun reduces the water it becomes saltier, salt gets raked out, then dried. Wind, sun, and sea. Those are the ingredients. There

are natural minerals—magnesium, calcium, and potassium, for instance—that result in delicious flavor. I love the simplicity and that it's been made there that way since the fourteenth century—maybe millennia. Trapani Sale di Gucciardo is my favorite, but don't obsess over a brand. Try a few and settle on your favorite affordable option.

People make claims about how salt affects baking—that it impedes fermentation, strengthens or preserves dough. I'll say this. I was working with my client Atte. Pizzeria Napoletana in Buenos Aires, Argentina. We'd made dough and left it out at room temperature. I told my client to put the dough in the fridge in the morning—when it should have doubled in size and be proofed—to slow it down. I get a call late morning—they'd arrived hours late and the dough had blown up and looked unusable. That didn't sound right, but when I arrived, bubbles were erupting. It *did* look unusable. They weren't late enough to make such a difference. It didn't add up.

We were on a forty-eight-hour cycle, and if we had to toss this batch we'd have to switch to a twenty-four-hour cycle to catch up (a benefit of a forty-eight-hour cycle—if something goes wrong, you have time to adjust).

We barely got the dough out of the tray (it almost degassed at the touch), but I made a pizza and, when I tasted it, I immediately knew the problem. They'd forgotten the salt. This is why I have clients follow the plan while I'm around—so they can make mistakes and I can troubleshoot as part of the learning process. This dough guy will never forget salt and the client will learn how to troubleshoot dough.

So salt *does* slow fermentation and strengthen dough.

Many of my recipes call for 3% salt. That's high. Some people go as low as half a percent. Many do up to 2.8%, but 3% slows fermentation and makes the crust taste amazing. There's also a debate about whether it's best to add salt with your first mix or second mix. I don't see a difference, so I recommend blending with the flour on first mix so you don't forget to add it.

DARTBOARD PIZZA

If there's one thing I hate it's something I call dartboard pizza.

I like simple pizzerias, and you don't see this at mom-and-pop, old-school Italian pizzerias. But in today's pizza world, there are people who use good ingredients, maybe a wood oven, and feel the need to make things fancy. They throw a bunch of ingredients at a pizza that sound nice but don't have a story of why they're together.

Why are these ingredients on this pizza? Who is the main character? Butternut squash, artichoke, heirloom tomato, roasted mushrooms, Kalamata olives—what do they have in common? Nothing. Some of their peak seasons are completely different. Don't dartboard pizza.

Start with a main character. Everything should support that. The main character will be determined by the best-looking thing at the market. It doesn't have to be fresh veg. Say you have beautiful heritage-breed pork. The pork fat should shine and everything should support it.

The Ancient Art of *Spulacci*

Okay, *spulacci* is a fake Italian word I made up for "splotchy sauce." It's just a great technique and I wanted to name it. I love old-school pizzerias. One of them, De Lorenzo's in Robbinsville, New Jersey (outside of Trenton), owned by Sam Amico, places mozzarella on the dough first, then splotches sauce on top. They have a cup and a spoon they use to *boom, boom, boom*, dab sauce on the mozzarella. I love that splotchy technique. Try it for yourself and see how a simple change in topping order can result in different flavor and texture dynamics.

AIRPLANE WING

WELL DEFINED CRUST

How to Open Up Dough

You've made your perfect dough, your oven is raging, and toppings are prepped. Time to open your dough. I use the same method for my New York–style, Thin & Crispy, and Neapolitanish pizzas (Tokyo-style is an exception).

Step One.

Remove the dough from the tray carefully to maintain its round integrity. Drop the bottom into some bench flour, move the dough to your work surface, then sprinkle flour on top.

Step Two.

Define the crust. I do this with my fingertips (no fingernails, please) to create a channel just inside the outer edge. The distance between the channel and edge will determine crust size. For a big crust, start a channel farther from the edge. For a small crust, closer. Once you have a channel of pressed dough that forms a circle inside the edge, you have a defined crust. Be careful not to press the crust—it won't bounce back.

Step Three.

After defining the crust, use your fingertips to gently but firmly press the center of the pizza, pushing down but not stretching it out. At this point, the dough's general shape will be established—a crust around the outside and an even, flat area for topping in the center. Be careful to not fall into the "airplane wing" trap (see diagram on page 37).

Step Four.

Now you can stretch the dough to its final shape. There are many methods, but I start by passing the dough back and forth between my hands while spinning it toward myself. Then I'll either put the dough on my fist and make a motion like turning a steering wheel, or toss it in the air, spinning it off the backs of my hands.

Step Five.

It's important to lay the dough flat to check your progress, especially if you're unsure about whether things are getting out of hand. Look for thin spots, and sprinkle the bottom of the pizza with flour and rub it in gently to eliminate sticky spots. Once you're happy with the shape, put it on your peel and shimmy it before topping it. If it doesn't shimmy freely, flip it and rub in another sprinkling of flour. If it's moving smoothly, top with intention posthaste.

FRESH MOZZA-RELLA

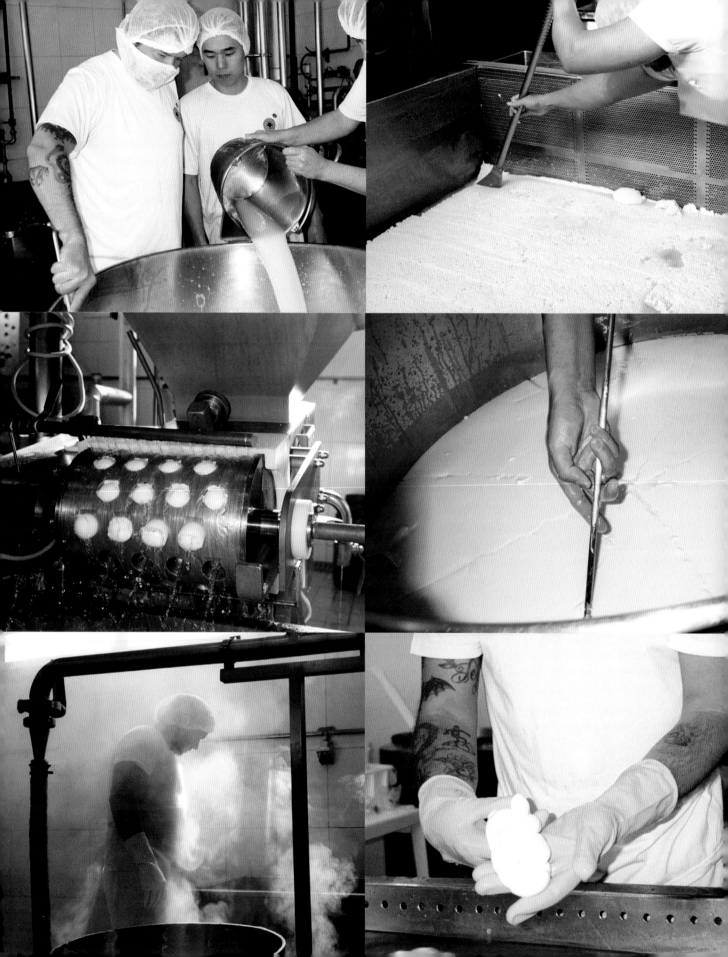

Equipment You'll Need for Fresh Mozzarella

Large Steel Mixing Bowl
Mozzarella Paddle (or Wooden Spoon)
Large Pot to Heat Water
Nitrile Gloves
Second Large Steel Mixing Bowl or
Medium-sized, Deep Container

I'M GOING TO TEACH YOU TWO WAYS TO MAKE YOUR OWN MOZZARELLA.

ONE'S EASY IF YOU'RE IN NORTH AMERICA, EVEN EASIER IF YOU'RE ON THE EAST COAST: STRETCHING MOZZARELLA FROM CURD. THE OTHER'S SLIGHTLY MORE DIFFICULT BUT CAN BE DONE ANYWHERE THERE'S RAW MILK. THE PAYOFF? BEAUTIFULLY SEASONED, FRESH, WARM MOZZARELLA—ONE OF THE BEST THINGS EVER.

stretching fresh mozzarella curd

Stretching your own mozzarella is fun, you get the creamiest, most delicious mozzarella you've ever had, and you can season it however you want. Freshly made mozzarella works on all kinds of pizza styles, and I've encouraged the practice at many restaurants.

At Upside Pizza in Times Square, we mix homemade cheese with traditional low-moisture aged mozzarella. The result is familiar and old-school. New things always come out of doing it too. At Marquee Pizzeria, a client in Iowa I taught to stretch fresh mozzarella for pizza, they let some set up in a third pan, then slice off big bricks, bread and deep-fry them, and serve them on arrabbiata sauce with Parmigiano-Reggiano, lemon zest, pepper, and fresh basil. It's called Brick O Mozza. It's the best fried mozzarella you'll ever have, and it starts with homemade cheese.

You'll need to use gloves—the mozzarella will be very hot. I find the fit of vinyl weird, and some people are allergic to latex, so I recommend nitrile (synthetic rubber). While some people are allergic to this too, it's less common, and the gloves come in black, so they look cool.

This recipe yields a pound of mozzarella. You can easily scale up depending on what you need.

> **453 g (1 pound) mozzarella curd**
> **16 grams sea salt (or 17 grams kosher salt)**
> **2 liters (8½ cups) water**
> **32 grams (¼ cup) ice**

1. Bring the curd to room temperature by leaving it out for at least 5 hours or overnight.

2. In a large, steel mixing bowl, break up the curd by hand into quarter-sized pieces. Rub the salt into the broken-up curds.

3. In a large pot, heat enough water to cover the curds to near boiling. Note: This does *not* mean you should put the curds in the pot before heating the water!

4. When the water reaches 186°F (86°C), pour the water over the salted curds in the steel mixing bowl. Move the curds around gently with a paddle or wooden spoon. When the curds start to "go plastic" by connecting and forming long protein chains, slowly lift them starting from the bottom of the bowl, stretching them until the consistency is smooth.

5. Once the curds come together and are stretching easily, pour out the warm water into another large bowl and add the ice to the warm water. The idea is to bring the water down to 85°F to 100°F (29°C to 38°C) for resting the mozzarella. Keep in mind that very cold water will shock the mozzarella and result in an unwanted tough texture.

6. Once the mozzarella is drained of the water, continue to stretch it. Taste it. It should be on point.

7. Once the surface of the mozzarella has a shiny smooth look, form it into the desired shape and size and rest it in the liquid poured off into the bowl with ice.

8. After 20 to 30 minutes, transfer the mozzarella into the container and let it reach room temperature (about 1½ hours), then wrap tightly in plastic wrap and refrigerate for serving.

9. The mozzarella is best used within 48 hours.

Where to Get Curd

Specialty cheese places that make mozzarella often have curd. If you live in a place with a healthy Italian-American community, you can sometimes convince an Italian deli or importer to sell you some. You can score it at Restaurant Depot (a national wholesale cash-and-carry foodservice supplier) and online from various suppliers, and even Amazon.

raw milk mozzarella

Makes 2 6-ounce (170-g) balls or
12 ounces (340 g)

If you want to make *great* mozz from scratch, find raw milk. It's not easy and could require ingenuity at a farmer's market. If you can't get raw milk, use low-temperature pasteurized, non-homogenized milk. Don't make it with milk in your fridge—it's not worth the effort. Just buy local mozzarella. If you *can* find some, the result will be life-changing.

You *will* need rennet and pH strips. Rennet is curdled milk that contains the enzyme rennin. I get mine from New York City's famous spice store Kalustyan's, which also sells it online, or you can order rennet from cheese-making websites. You can find pH strips online for under $15.

3.78 L (1 gallon) raw milk
7 ml (1½ tsp) citric acid dissolved in
60 ml (¼ cup) water
1.2 ml (¼ tsp) liquid rennet dissolved
in 60 ml (¼ cup) water
14 grams (2½ teaspoons) kosher salt

1. In a large non-reactive pot, combine the milk and citric acid solution. Over low heat, warm the milk to 90°F (32°C). You're aiming for a pH of 5.1 to 5.4.

2. Remove from heat and add the liquid rennet solution. Whisk for 10 seconds, cover, and let sit for 15 minutes.

3. Test the curd by running a knife in along the edge of the pot and see if it easily pulls away from the sides. It should be the consistency of silken tofu. If it's not quite there, recover and let sit for another 5 to 10 minutes.

4. While still in the pot, use a long knife to cut a grid in the curd. The cubes should be about 1 by 1 inch (2½ by 2½ cm). Make sure you're cutting all the way to the bottom of the pot.

5. Return the pot to low heat and bring the temperature up to 105°F (40°C). Remove from heat and allow to sit for another 5 minutes, uncovered.

6. The whey (a yellow liquid) will start to separate from the cut curds. Using a colander set over a large bowl, drain out the whey and carefully press out as much liquid as you can from the curds. Let the curds rest for thirty minutes. The curds will have formed a large mass at this point.

7. Bring about a quart of water to 185°F (85°C). Meanwhile, in a metal bowl, weigh the curd. It should be about 12 ounces (340 g).

8. Sprinkle your salt over the curds and add enough 185°F (85°C) water to just cover. Put on a pair of food-safe gloves (I recommend nitrile gloves) and begin to stretch the curd, lifting it above the bowl and letting gravity pull the curd back to the hot water. If the curd doesn't stretch easily, add more hot water. Continue this process until the cheese is shiny and smooth; it should only take a minute or so.

9. It is important to note that the more the cheese is stretched, the more moisture it will lose and the stiffer it will be.

10. Form your cheese into your desired shape and size and transfer to a 70°F (30°C) bowl of water. Taste the mozzarella and if it needs more seasoning, lightly salt the water. Let rest for about 30 minutes.

11. Immediately after removing the mozzarella from the water, use it on a pizza or serve warm. Any leftovers can be stored in the fridge, wrapped tightly in plastic, or fully submerged in water.

I'm often asked about using fresh or canned tomatoes. For sauce, canned is better. Chances are, no matter when you make pizza, it won't be tomato season. If you can get great in-season tomatoes there are better ways to use them on pizza.

Many people don't know that the plum tomato (like the famous San Marzano), the tomato most prized for Italian-style tomato sauces, was bred to be packed. In fact, many Italians and Italian-Americans still buy tomatoes in bulk in summer and jar them for the rest of the year. According to David Gentilcore's **Pomodoro! A History of the Tomato in Italy**, the modern variety of the plum tomato (the "square tomato") is bred to be low to the ground for harvesting machines and yield. The rise of the tomato and the rise of food industrialization in Italy are linked, it seems.

Canning isn't exactly modern technology, but paired with the rise of the tomato, it had profound effects on Southern Italy, creating a food staple for the poor. When you think of Italian red sauce, you're talking about Southern Italian cuisine, and that tomato sauce is available year-round because they're canning and jarring. It allowed them to stretch a little meat and vegetables and create delicious things. Take a piece of bread, add tomato and olive oil, and you have a meal. It transformed the region and led to Italian-American cuisine.

In America, the players in Italian-style tomatoes are California, New Jersey, and imported Italian tomatoes. If you get the best canned tomatoes from Italy, they will be amazing—maybe better than the best Californian tomato. But chances of getting them are low.

Among many misconceptions is that pizza requires sauce made with many ingredients cooked a secret amount of time. The best pizza sauces (and the best pizza, generally) are made using raw tomato sauce, meaning canned tomatoes seasoned with salt or salt and olive oil.

The best tomatoes for a raw sauce for New York– or Neapolitan-style pizza are whole peeled tomatoes packed with basil, citric acid, and salt. You can choose one without basil, but my favorites happen to have basil. Avoid calcium chloride—it makes tomatoes firm but inhibits a smooth puree. For more information about choosing the right canned tomatoes, see the "Products" section on page **242**.

basic tomato sauce

Makes 1 quart (about 1 liter)

There's this notion that seeds make sauce bitter. I've made a lot of sauce using a food mill. The idea is tomatoes pass through, seeds get caught, and you get a seedless sauce that isn't bitter and has great texture. Food mills are great, but when hand-cranking became a full-time job, we experimented with an immersion blender. Side-by-side there was no bitterness. I think the gelatinous sacs surrounding tomato seeds (which inhibit germination) add *more* flavor. Either way, if you get good tomatoes, bitterness won't be a problem. Start with great product and you won't have to try to fix bad ingredients.

1 (794-gram/28-ounce) can whole peeled tomatoes (preferably Bianco DiNapoli), drained
5 grams (about 1 teaspoon) sea salt, adjust to taste
10 grams (about 2 teaspoons) extra-virgin olive oil, adjust to taste
Combine the drained tomatoes and salt in a large bowl.

1. In a bowl, combine the tomatoes, salt, and olive oil.

2. With an immersion blender, blend until the tomatoes are smooth and sauce is emulsified.

3. Taste and adjust the seasoning. Refrigerate until ready to use; best if used same day (after 2 days, I recommend not using it as it will be considerably less good).

Determining Your Go-To Tomato

Buy all the whole peeled tomatoes available, taste them, then use the best one! What are we looking for? A balance of acidity and sweetness with little bitterness. When you look at canned tomatoes for quality, one thing you can do is open the can, drain it, and then wash off the "sauce" the tomatoes are sitting in. If they're red and fully ripened, you've got a packer discerning about quality. If some are yellow or green, bruised, or dark red, the canner is throwing in anything. Quality is not a priority.

tomato flavor bomb AND robust tomato sauce

Makes 1 quart (about 1 liter)

This is a great way to add a ton of flavor to a sauce without cooking down huge batches of tomato sauce forever. It's easy and will make any room it's cooked in smell incredible. It always reminds me of walking into the kitchen with Sunday sauce going. Add a little to basic tomato sauce for increased depth of flavor.

15 to 20 cloves garlic, peeled, or about 50 grams

1 sprig rosemary

2 sprigs basil

2 sprigs thyme

1 (794-gram/28-ounce) can whole peeled tomatoes (preferably Bianco DiNapoli), drained

5 grams (about a teaspoon) sea salt

Pinch sugar or drizzle of honey (optional)

220 to 440 grams (1 to 2 cups) extra-virgin olive oil

1. Preheat the oven to 425°F (218°C).

2. Cover the bottom of a high sided, oven-safe pan with the garlic and herbs. Completely cover them with the tomatoes, arranged in one flat layer. Press down to remove as much air as possible. Evenly sprinkle the salt and sugar (if using) over the tomatoes.

3. Add enough of the olive oil to completely cover the tomatoes. If needed, gently push the tomatoes down with the back of a spoon.

4. Bake for 30 minutes, or until the garlic is completely soft. Carefully remove the pan from the oven; the oil will be very hot. Let it cool for 30 minutes.

5. Drain excess oil and remove the herbs. Refrigerate and reserve for another use.

6. Using an immersion blender, puree the tomato and garlic mixture until smooth and emulsified (it will be very orange because of the oil). Taste and adjust the seasoning.

7. Refrigerate until ready to use or up to 3 days.

8. You can integrate this at 10% to the Basic Tomato Sauce recipe (page 52) to up the flavor. Now it's **Robust Tomato Sauce**.

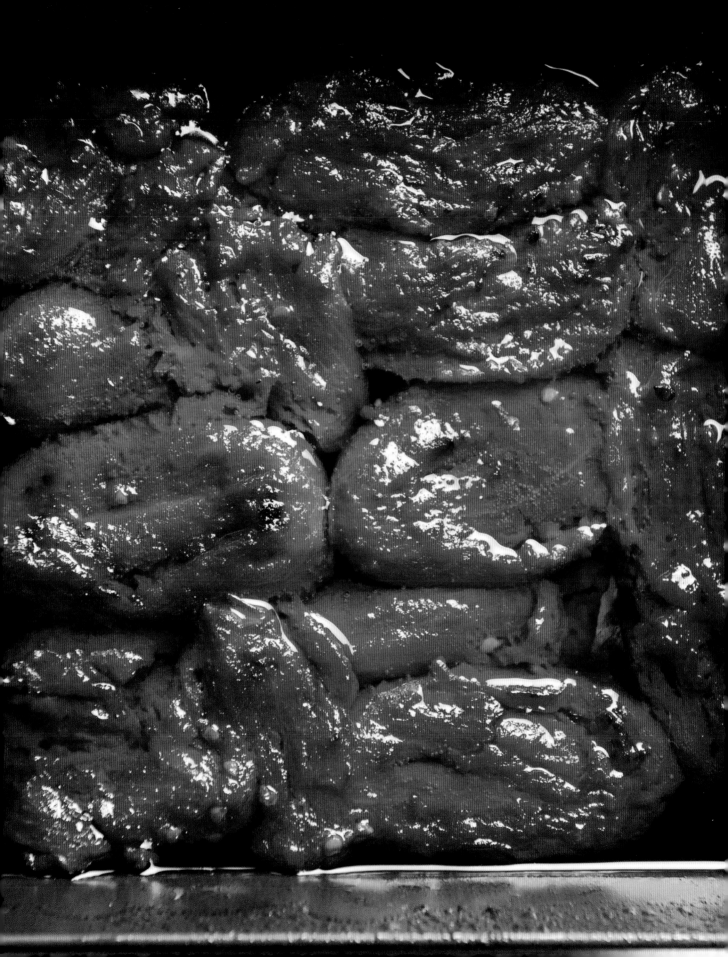

spicy grandma sauce

Makes 1 quart (about 1 liter)

This is based on the sauce I learned from my grandma. She likes spicy things. Hey, Sicilians living in Texas—we're down with spice. Think of it like an *arrabbiata* sauce but nobody's angry.

**1 (794-gram/28-ounce)
can whole peeled tomatoes
(preferably Bianco DiNapoli), drained**

4 grams (1 teaspoon) kosher salt

**110 grams (½ cup) extra-virgin olive oil,
plus more if needed**

**40 grams (about 1½ ounces)
yellow onion, thinly sliced**

30 grams (5 cloves) garlic, chopped

**14 grams (about 4) fresh red chiles
(bird's-eye or similar), thinly sliced**

**8 grams (about 3) dried
Calabrian chiles**

**10 grams (about ⅓ ounce) basil,
chopped**

1. Put the tomatoes in a large bowl. Using your dominant hand, crush each tomato into walnut-sized pieces. Season with the salt and 55 grams (¼ cup) of the olive oil. Mix thoroughly and set aside.

2. In a medium sauté pan, heat the remaining 55 grams (¼ cup) oil over medium-high heat. Add the onion and cook until it begins to brown, about 10 minutes. Add the garlic and cook for an additional 2 minutes, or until the garlic is soft.

3. Add the fresh red chiles and Calabrian chiles and continue to cook. Raise the heat to high, add the tomatoes, and cook for 5 minutes, stirring vigorously. Add a bit more olive oil if the mixture begins sticking.

4. Add the basil, taste, and adjust the seasoning. Transfer to a container, cool, and refrigerate until ready to use. Use in first 2 days or freeze.

Calabrian Chile

Crushed pepper flakes, or crushed red pepper, will be familiar to any pizza lover as the little shaker of pulverized dried spicy red chiles that are left on the table along with oregano and parm for doctoring up your slice. In Italy it's known as pepperoncini and is a catch-all term for spicy chiles. But not all chile flakes are created equal. Calabria is especially obsessed with pepperoncini and is known for having the spiciest food in Italy, so it makes sense that the Calabrian chile is especially prized. I highly recommend leveling up from the packets of chile to dried Calabrian chile powder. I like the unique flavor, more intense heat, and the fine powder consistency. It makes a big difference in flavor so if you can find it, use it anywhere chile flakes are called for.

ESTABLISHING THE BASELINE

YOU'VE GOTTA START SIMPLE BEFORE YOU CAN GO CRAZY.

THIS THIN & CRISPY DOUGH RECIPE AND THE PIZZA RECIPES THAT USE IT REPRESENT WHAT I THINK OF AS AMERICA'S CLASSIC PIZZAS. I'M NOT ITALIAN AND THIS ISN'T AN ITALIAN COOKBOOK. I'M AN AMERICAN OF ITALIAN DESCENT AND THE PIZZA I GREW UP EATING WAS AMERICAN ITALIAN.

Home Oven Temperatures: Turn the Dial to 11

Most home ovens will never be hot enough to produce restaurant-quality pizza. They're going to be in the 450°F to 550°F (232°C to 288°C) range. Even when they say 550°F (288°C), they're not really 550°F. Tricking out your oven (see page 265) can get it into the 600°F (315°C) range. That's what I suggest doing for every recipe in this book. If you're using a conventional home oven that's not tricked out, turn it to its highest setting and allow it to reach temp for at least a half hour. Remember, the hotter the oven, the better the final product.

thin &
crispy dough

Makes 7 (250-gram) dough balls

500 grams high-protein bread flour
500 grams all-purpose flour
30 grams (about 1 ounce) sea salt
600 grams (2½ cups) water, at 72°F (22°C)
150 grams (about 5 ounces) starter (3 to 5 hours after feeding it at room temperature)
5 grams cake or fresh yeast (or 1.58 grams instant yeast)*
80 grams (5¾ cups) extra-virgin olive oil, plus more for the container

BAKER'S PERCENTAGES
100% flour
60% water
15% starter
8% extra-virgin olive oil
3% sea salt
0.5% yeast

*This dough works great with just all-natural leavening, but the addition of yeast will enhance the crispiness, so the yeast is optional

This is a simple recipe. It's wet and on the high end of salt and fat for pizza dough. By itself, this recipe could produce all kinds of results. The most important thing is methodology. When I'm training someone in the opening stages of building a dough program they'll often ask, "Is this step important?" or "Does it matter how I do this?"

Yes and no. Everything matters. It's all important. But is it *absolutely* the right way? No. Everything is flexible. You need a recipe *and* a methodology. And you need to employ them *intentionally*. Sometimes a methodology has to strike a balance between quality, volume, and consistency. It's important to have a standard operating procedure but also a culture that allows a recipe and methodology to adapt.

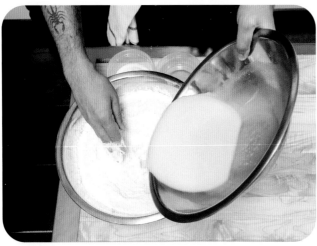

1. Weigh all the ingredients in separate containers. In a large mixing bowl, combine the flours and salt and mix thoroughly with clean hands.

2. In another large mixing bowl, combine the water, starter, and yeast.

3. Create a crater in the flour and pour the liquid mixture in the center. Begin mixing with your dominant hand. Start in the center of the bowl and mix in a clockwise fashion until the dough comes together into a ball and the bowl is clean. After it has just come together, add the olive oil and mix until fully combined. Stop mixing and cover the bowl with plastic wrap. Rest for 30 minutes.

4. Uncover the dough and mix by stretching and folding the dough onto itself for 5 minutes.

5. Lightly oil a large container. Add the dough and cover tightly with plastic wrap. Allow the dough to rest for 2 hours at room temperature. Then gently fold the dough into itself. Re-wrap and let it sit at room temperature for about 3 hours.

6. Remove the dough and place it on a lightly floured surface. Lightly flour your hands and, using a dough cutter and scale, portion it into 250-gram dough balls. Form each dough into a tight ball by folding it in on itself, being careful to handle the ball quickly and gently to not transfer much heat.

7. Place the balls on a lightly floured 13-by-18-inch (33-by-46-cm) baking sheet. Lightly flour the surface of the dough balls and cover them with plastic wrap. Proof at room temperature for 5 hours or until the balls double in size. At this point you can use them or transfer to the refrigerator and rest for up to 48 hours.

tomato pie

Makes 1 (13-inch/33-cm) pizza

---

1 (250-g) Thin & Crispy dough ball (page 63)
84 grams (6 tablespoons) Robust Tomato Sauce (page 54)
Pinch dried wild Sicilian oregano, stems removed
50 grams (about 1¾ ounces) Pecorino-Romano, finely grated
14 grams (1 tablespoon) extra-virgin olive oil, in a squeeze bottle

The tomato pie is the American version of the Neapolitan marinara pizza. If you go to New Haven (if you haven't, go), you're getting a tomato pie. Then there's the New Jersey tomato pie, one of the oldest pizzeria traditions in America (De Lorenzo's Tomato Pies in Robbinsville, New Jersey, is my go-to). The tomato pie is making a comeback, and it's something that lets great ingredients shine. So much pizza is laden with mozzarella, so let's sing the praises of a lightly cheesed pie.

1. Preheat the oven with pizza stones to your oven's highest temperature setting (usually 550°F/288°C).

2. Stretch out the dough according to the Thin & Crispy method (see page 38).

3. Using a ladle or a large spoon, spread the sauce evenly on the dough starting from the inside out, leaving 1 inch (2½ cm) around the dough's circumference for the crust. Dust with the oregano.

4. Evenly top the pizza with 30 grams (about 1 ounce) of the Pecorino and, using a squeeze bottle, a drizzle of 5 grams (a scant tablespoon) of the olive oil.

5. Bake the pizza directly on the pizza stone for 5½ minutes, or until the crust is nicely browned, checking the bottom and rotating it halfway through for an evenly colored crust.

6. Cut the pizza into six slices and top the pizza with the remaining Pecorino and olive oil.

the original (plain cheese)

Makes 1 (13-inch/33-cm) pizza

---

1 (250-g) Thin & Crispy dough ball (page 63)
56 grams (¼ cup) Robust Tomato Sauce (page 54)
Pinch dried wild Sicilian oregano, stems removed
3 basil leaves
50 grams (about 1¾ ounce) low-moisture mozzarella, shredded
60 grams (about 2⅛ ounces) fresh mozzarella
5 grams (1 teaspoon) extra-virgin olive oil, in a squeeze bottle
20 grams (about ¾ ounce) Parmigiano-Reggiano, finely grated

It's called The Original for a reason. To me, the quintessential American classic is a plain cheese pizza from a classic New York City pizzeria. Whether it's the Original Ray's, the Original Tony's, the Original Luigi's, or the Original . . . *whatever*, this recipe conjures that feeling you get when you order a cheese slice, add oregano, chile flakes, and a little funky Parm on top, and it all comes together with the right balance of crust, sauce, and stringy mozzarella—where the cheese and tomato adhere to the crust in a blend that becomes something more than the sum of parts. *That's* the nostalgic American pizza I'm going after here.

1. Preheat the oven with pizza stones to your oven's highest temperature setting (usually 550°F/288°C).

2. Stretch out the dough according to the Thin & Crispy method (see page 38).

3. Using a 2-ounce (60-ml) ladle or a large spoon, spread the sauce evenly on the dough starting from the inside out, leaving 1 inch (2½ cm) around the dough's circumference for the crust. Dust with the oregano. Tear the basil leaves into small coin sized pieces and evenly distribute them atop the sauce.

4. Distribute the low-moisture mozzarella evenly onto the sauce.

5. Using your fingers, tear off quarter-sized pieces of fresh mozzarella and top directly onto the pizza, leaving about ¾ inch (2 cm) between each piece.

6. Bake the pizza directly on the pizza stone for 5½ minutes, or until the crust is nicely browned, checking the bottom and rotating it halfway through for an evenly colored crust.

7. Cut the pizza into 6 slices. Using a squeeze bottle, evenly top the pizza with the olive oil and then the Parmigiano-Reggiano.

Pizza

sausage & pepper pizza

Makes 1 (13-inch/33-cm) pizza

1 (250-g) Thin & Crispy dough ball
(page 63)

30 grams (about 1 ounce)
low-moisture mozzarella, shredded

30 grams (about 1 ounce) caciocavallo
or provolone cheese, shredded

56 grams (¼ cup)
Robust Tomato Sauce (page 54)

40 grams (about 1½ ounces)
Roasted Peppers (page 224)

30 grams (about 1 ounce)
Falco Sausage (page 211)

25 grams (about 1 ounce)
Pecorino-Romano, finely grated

The key to a great sausage pie is great sausage. And the key to great sausage is making it yourself with the best, freshest, just-ground pork. I recommend pasture-raised—a heritage breed like a Duroc, Berkshire, or Red Wattle. If you go to a whole-animal butcher, they'll usually be grinding shoulder for ground pork to make sausage and will have some. Anywhere I go, I say, "If we're doing pork sausage, we're starting with the best pork you can get, and from there, we're seasoning simply."

A dry-spice blend, a little garlic, and white wine—but it's all about fennel, black pepper, chile, salt, and if you want, a little sugar. You have it all in a big chunk, you portion it out raw onto the pizza before you bake it, the fat melts as the sausage tightens up in the oven and seeps into the cheese. It's gonna be great. And then you get the sweetness—and sometimes the heat—of the peppers . . . it's a classic Italian-American combination. I love the balance between the sausage's savoriness, sweetness, and fattiness and the acidity of the pickled peppers.

1. Preheat the oven with pizza stones to your oven's highest temperature setting (usually 550°F/288°C).

2. Stretch out the dough according to the Thin & Crispy method (see page 38).

3. Top the pizza with the mozzarella slices, working from the outside in and trying to cover most of the dough, but leaving 1 inch (2½ cm) around the dough's circumference for the crust. Using the shredded caciocavallo or provolone, fill in the gaps where there is no cheese.

4. Using a 2-ounce (60-ml) ladle or a large spoon, spread the sauce from the outside in using the *spulacci* technique (see page 37).

5. Evenly top the pizza with roasted peppers strips (don't clump them together!).

6. Using your fingers (I recommend wearing nitrile gloves), pluck off coin sized balls of raw sausage and place them evenly on top of the pizza.

7. Bake the pizza directly on the pizza stone for 5½ minutes, or until the crust is nicely browned, checking the bottom and rotating it halfway through for an evenly colored crust.

8. Cut the pizza into 6 slices and top with the Pecorino-Romano.

the new york–style margherita pizza

Makes 1 (13-inch/33-cm) pizza

1 (250-g) Thin & Crispy dough ball (page 63)
90 grams (about 3 ounces) fresh mozzarella, hand-sliced as thin as possible
56 grams (¼ cup) Basic Tomato Sauce (page 52)
Pinch dried wild Sicilian oregano, stems removed
3 basil leaves
25 grams (about 1 ounce) Parmigiano-Reggiano, finely grated
5 grams (1 teaspoon) extra-virgin olive oil, in a squeeze bottle

This pizza tries to recapture the feeling of the first time I had a mind-blowingly good old-school New York City–style coal-oven pizza. My dad took me to Patsy's in DUMBO in the '90s when it was still called Patsy's. No shredded cheese—this was fresh mozzarella topped with sauce, a drizzle of olive oil, basil, and a hint of oregano.

That combination and process (fresh mozz on the bottom, topped with an uncooked, plain sauce) are magical. The coal oven places—Patsy's, Grimaldi's, and Totonno's—*that's* what the New York–style Margherita represents to me. It's about getting the right thickness of mozzarella and the right oven temperature. You want it on the higher end because if you cook too long the cheese overcooks and you lose the freshness of the sauce. *Semplice è difficile.* Simple is difficult.

1. Preheat the oven with pizza stones to your oven's highest temperature setting (usually 550°F/288°C).

2. Stretch out the dough according to the Thin & Crispy method (see page 38).

3. Lay the sliced mozzarella onto the pizza with about 1 inch (2½ cm) between the slices, but leaving 1 inch (2½ cm) around the dough's circumference for the crust.

4. With a 2-ounce (60-ml) ladle or a large spoon, spread the sauce from the outside in using the *spulacci* technique (see page 37). Dust with the oregano. Tear the basil leaves into small pieces and evenly distribute them atop the sauce.

5. Sprinkle half of the Parmigiano-Reggiano over the entire pizza and, using a squeeze bottle, drizzle with the olive oil, working from the outside in.

6. Bake the pizza directly on the pizza stone for 5½ minutes, or until the crust is nicely browned, checking the bottom and rotating it halfway through for an evenly colored crust.

7. Cut the pizza into 6 slices and top with the remaining Parmigiano.

Sausage: Crumbled versus Medallions

I *don't* like cased sausage medallions on pizza. I won't order a medallion-topped slice. Medallions get cooked twice, once before being added pre-cook, and again in the oven. So they're dry. They also make for unwieldy bites. If you're making homemade sausage, you don't want to spend all that time to turn it into something dry and unappealing. You'd be filling casing just to squeeze it out. That's silly. Loose sausage you can tear into crumbles distribute flavors better and *looks* better. That's the way to go. Trust me.

Cupping Pepperoni

Even if you're unfamiliar with the term, you've probably still seen cupping pepperoni. Cupping pepperoni is simply pepperoni in a casing that contracts when cooked. The pepperoni cups and little grease puddles form. Ezzo Sausage Company, who I've partnered with in the past, makes one of the best. It's smaller in diameter but available in different sizes. Ezzo's does baby cuppers 41 millimeters, 51 millimeters (the most popular size), and 79 millimeters (jumbos), which remind me of chain delivery pizza pepperoni. Ezzo Supreme pepperoni burns charcoal black around the edges and is spicy, whereas Ezzo's GiAntonio pepperoni has a lighter brown edge. I like the 41-millimeter GiAntonios—they cup nicely.

PEPPERONI

I have a funny relationship with pepperoni. Being raised vegetarian, I first tasted it at twenty-six at Adrienne's Pizzabar in New York City's Financial District. It was the cupping variety. I loved the crunchy curled edges and the smokiness with fennel sausage. Things went downhill.

As I tried more pepperoni, it got worse. The flat stuff lacks texture, is too processed, and has a chemical flavor. Without a nostalgic taste for it, how could it compete with the hot *soppressata* and other cured meats that I was topping pizzas with? I avoided it.

Fast-forward to Hurricane Irene in 2011. The day after, we wanted to open Roberta's for the Bushwick community. Things went great until we noticed soppressata was low, and deliveries wouldn't arrive for days. I sent a bike delivery person across the Williamsburg Bridge to Salumeria Biellese (one of America's best Italian-American salumerias) for more. Only one stick of soppressata was available, but they had plenty of pepperoni.

At the time, pepperoni wasn't used at the restaurant, but I said, "Fuck it, Biellese wouldn't make bad pepperoni—they have that Slow Food snail!" So, the pepperoni arrives, we slice it thin and throw it on a pizza. It's not a cupping pepperoni, so the edges aren't crunchy, but there is crispness and amazing flavor. It tasted exactly how American pepperoni should taste, but with quality ingredients.

Since then I've discovered Ezzo Sausage Company cupping pepperoni. Ezzo is an awesome old-school family-run operation. These guys have been in business for over forty years. It's the gold standard for cupping pepperoni. I hope more producers will give this Italian-American pizza contribution the respect it deserves.

I've found the addition of jalapeño makes pepperoni shine. That spicy, smoky, acidic, fatty combo is the new American classic pizza combination. And I'm not ashamed to admit, as a proud Texan, that I'm dipping in ranch dressing. Not any ranch—I've got the perfect ranch designed for dipping pizza, in particular Pepperoni and Pickled Chile Pizza (see next page).

Pizza

pepperoni AND pickled chile pizza

Makes 1 (13-inch/33-cm) pizza

---

1 (250-g) Thin & Crispy dough ball (page 63)
56 grams (¼ cup) Basic Tomato Sauce (page 52)
55 grams (about 2 ounces) low-moisture mozzarella, shredded
60 grams (about 2 ounces) pepperoni, sliced (about 25 pieces)
30 grams (about 1 ounce) Pickled Chiles (page 219)
25 grams (about 1 ounce) Pecorino-Romano, finely grated
Pinch dried wild Sicilian oregano, stems removed

Pepperoni pizza is arguably the modern American classic. To me, *this* is the new classic. As you may have already read here, I didn't grow up eating pepperoni, but I was raised eating lots of pickled chiles. To me, it's about the combination. Pepperoni is great, but it can be just one note and, frankly, boring solo, even the best stuff. In my mind, you *have* to add jalapeños.

1. Preheat the oven with pizza stones to your oven's highest temperature setting (usually 550°F/288°C).

2. Stretch out the dough according to the Thin & Crispy method (see page 38).

3. Using a 2-ounce (60-ml) ladle or a large spoon, spread the sauce evenly on the dough starting from the inside out, leaving 1 inch (2½ cm) around the dough's circumference for the crust.

4. Distribute the mozzarella evenly onto the sauce.

5. Place the pepperoni evenly on the pizza, starting from the outside in. Remember: Pepperoni migration is unavoidable! Don't be surprised post-bake if they aren't where you left them.

6. Bake the pizza directly on the pizza stone for 5½ minutes, or until the crust is nicely browned, checking the bottom and rotating it halfway through for an evenly colored crust.

7. Cut the pizza into 6 slices and top with the pickled chiles and Pecorino-Romano. Sprinkle with oregano.

palace special pizza

Makes 1 (13-inch/33-cm) pizza

I was working with Marquee Pizzeria in Coralville, Iowa, and we kept driving by this place, A & A Pagliai's Pizza. The old-school sign was so awesome (signs are important) I had to go. With respect to Pagliai's history (they opened their first pizzeria in 1957), the pizza was basically your classic Midwest tavern-style—crispy and loaded with toppings. Pagliai's supreme (topped with sausage, beef, pepperoni, mushroom, and onion) is the "Palace Special." It's a cool name for a supreme. Shout-out to Pagliai's.

1 (250-g) Thin & Crispy dough ball
(page 63)

56 grams (¼ cup)
Robust Tomato Sauce (page 54)

30 grams (about 1 ounce)
low-moisture mozzarella, shredded

60 grams (about 2 ounces) pepperoni,
sliced (about 25 pieces)

30 grams (about 1 ounce)
Falco Sausage (page 211)

20 grams (about ¾ ounce) red onion,
thinly sliced

30 grams (about 1 ounce)
Pickled Chiles (page 219)

25 grams (about 1 ounce)
Pecorino-Romano, finely grated

Pinch dried wild Sicilian oregano,
stems removed

1. Preheat the oven with pizza stones to your oven's highest temperature setting (usually 550°F/288°C).

2. Stretch out the dough according to the Thin & Crispy method (see page 38).

3. Using a 2-ounce (60-ml) ladle or a large spoon, spread the sauce evenly on the dough starting from the inside out, leaving 1 inch (2½ cm) around the dough's circumference for the crust.

4. Distribute the mozzarella evenly onto the sauce.

5. Place the pepperoni evenly on the pizza, starting from the outside in. Remember: Pepperoni migration is unavoidable!

6. Using your fingers (I recommend wearing nitrile gloves), pluck off coin sized balls of sausage and place them evenly on top of the pizza. From the outside in, distribute the red onions among the pieces of sausage.

7. Bake the pizza directly on the pizza stone for 5½ minutes, or until the crust is nicely browned, checking the bottom and rotating it halfway through for an evenly colored crust.

8. Cut the pizza into 6 slices and top with the pickled chiles and Pecorino-Romano. Sprinkle with oregano.

Same (But Evolving) Pizza Chef, Different Pies

The pizza program I create for every client is unique. Styles aside, because of my approach to dough, using natural leavening and, for the most part, local flours, the pizzas are different depending on where I consult. Even if I *were* to do the exact same topping combinations (I don't), toppings are always local, and these local ingredients change the flavor profiles of even my most signature pies.

THE MILLENNIUM FALCO

I didn't personally name many of my early pizzas. Their naming involved lots of standing around. You'd come up with a pizza, everyone tasted it, and if it was liked, people threw out names. Ultimately, someone with authority would decide. That was it. Christened.

Ever since my first job, when people find out my last name, I'm just Falco. It's cool sounding, I guess, and easy to say in the heat of the moment. "Falco, you're about to burn those fries!"

I have a healthy ego, but I also respond to "Dude," and wouldn't name pizzas after myself. In this case, I didn't. I came up with the pizza, and someone was like, "Why don't you call it the Millennium Falco?" I'm a Star Wars nerd, so I liked that. I called my dad and grandma and told them a pizza with our name was on the menu. I was proud.

The Millennium Falco was a crowd-pleaser from the beginning and many people have told me it's their favorite pizza.

I've tweaked it over the years. And since my first international pizza making experiences, people have asked me to do versions. At a pop-up in Brazil, I was asked for a take on it and said the way I like the Falco is with pickled jalapeños. Thus was born Señor Falco. I've done it with caramelized onions, subbed mushrooms for sausage (the Frank Falco because my father and son, both Franks, are vegetarians)—it's a versatile pie.

It's a calling card. As a tribute pizza or for projects I consult on, I offer the opportunity to do a new take on the Falco. Now it's been made all over the world, and every time with a different name and a unique twist to the ingredients.

the falco pizza

Makes 1 (13-inch/33-cm) pizza

My most well-known pizza. I've been riffing on it the world over. It's straight-up stolen from my great-grandmother. Breadcrumbs were a constant in her cooking. They're practical and symbolic. Great-grandma Lena made bread daily. By drying and blending the stale, left-over bread, you got the best breadcrumbs, a way to thicken sauce and add texture to dishes gratis. Nothing wasted.

The symbolism comes from Saint Joseph, whose feast day we celebrated with a meatless pasta of favas, fennel, and bread-crumbs, the last symbolizing sawdust in a carpenter's workshop. I was spared a lot of Catholic indoctrination, but I'm writing this at my desk by a glow-in-the-dark Virgin Mary that belonged to my grandfather, and I wear a Saint Christopher necklace because it was a gift, my father wears one, and it's supposed to protect the wearer while traveling. I don't put too much stock in it, but these connections are important (and I'll tell you this, if I open my own place it will be on a Tuesday because that superstition was passed to me too).

Religion and superstition aside, I use breadcrumbs in many pizzas. But on the Falco, they're the star. They're layered onto the sauce with a hard cheese and olive oil to create a magical "super sauce" that comes together in the oven. It's a balance some have difficulty recreating—too much, it's dry. Not enough? Too wet.

Without mozzarella, this pizza is nothing but full, maximum-strength, *nonna mamma mia* vibes. It's a Sicilian flavor profile punch in the mouth.

1 (250-g) Thin & Crispy dough ball (page 63)

84 grams (6 tablespoons) Basic Tomato Sauce (page 52)

Pinch Calabrian chile flakes

6 grams (about ¼ ounce) Sourdough Breadcrumbs (page 226)

30 grams (about 1 ounce) caciocavallo, finely grated

25 grams (about 1 ounces) Parmigiano-Reggiano, finely grated

20 grams (1½ tablespoons) extra-virgin olive oil, in a squeeze bottle

20 grams (about ¾ ounce) red onions, thinly sliced

1. Preheat the oven with pizza stones to your oven's highest temperature setting (usually 550°F/288°C).

2. Stretch out the dough according to the Thin & Crispy method (see page 38).

3. Using a ladle or a large spoon, spread the sauce onto the entire pizza, leaving about 1 inch (2½ cm) around the dough's circumference for the crust. Top with the chile flakes and dust with the breadcrumbs.

4. Follow with the caciocavallo and half of the Parmigiano-Reggiano and, using a squeeze bottle, a drizzle of olive oil.

5. Finish with the red onions.

6. Bake the pizza directly on the pizza stone for 5½ minutes, or until the crust is nicely browned, checking the bottom and rotating it halfway through for an evenly colored crust.

7. Cut the pizza into 6 slices and top with the remaining Parmigiano-Reggiano.

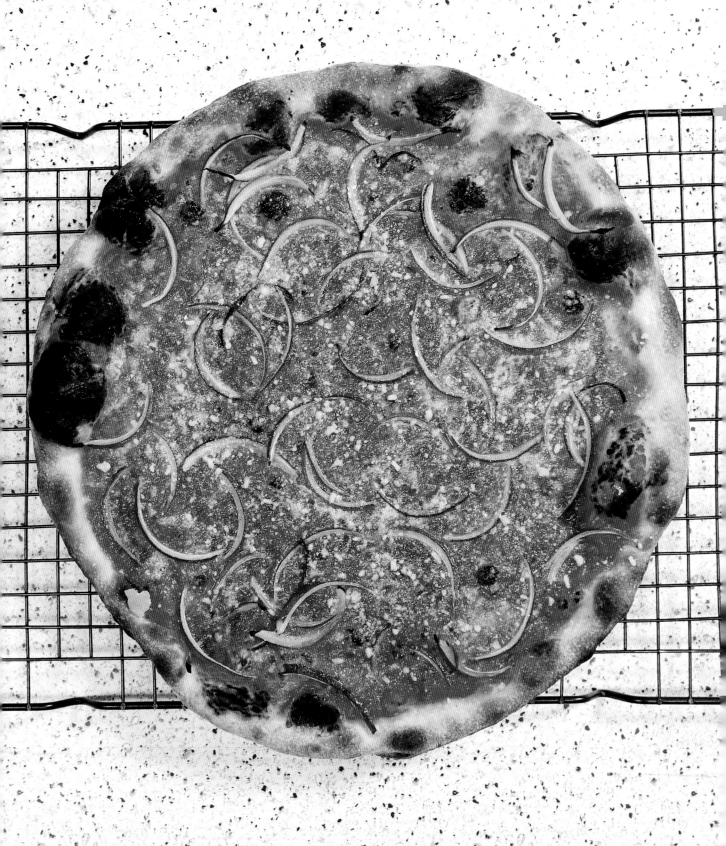

NEAPOLITANISH PIZZA

There's good news and bad news.

Bad news first: You can't make Neapolitan, Neo-Neapolitan, or whatever you want to call it in your home oven. Sorry, not gonna happen. You can hack your oven to get it hotter than it was made to, but you still won't be close to the 700°F (371°C) floor and 1,000°F (538°C) dome temperatures of a Neapolitan-style wood oven.

Sorry. YouTube lied. Other cookbooks lied. I'm *not* going to lie to you. Let's move on.

Ready for good news? There *are* things you can buy if you want to make the investment that will allow you to make Neapolitanish pizza. (I'm not touching VPN-certified Neapolitan pizza—there are too many rules, and it's not what I do.)

These recipes assume you have one of those hacked ovens (see page 265) or a wood oven. I encourage you to use a home high-temp oven like the Breville Smart Oven Pizzaiolo (I've partnered with Breville in the past), Roccbox, Ooni, Pavesi Bambino, or anything that gets super-hot. They'll all get you over that invisible boundary of 800°F (427°C) that will make your Neapolitanish pizza *mamma mia*. High temperature defines the style.

The reason New York–style pizza turned into a style different from early "Neapolitan" pizzas is that people started using gas deck ovens that cook at lower temperatures. This innovation is largely thanks to the inventor of the gas deck oven, Italian immigrant Frank Mastro, who should be credited as one of the people who helped spread pizza in general, and New York–style pizza specifically, out of Italian immigrant enclaves.

Vera Pizza Neapolitanish

The Associazione Verace Pizza Napoletana (True Neapolitan Pizza Association, or AVPN) is a nonprofit founded in Naples in 1984 to protect Verace Pizza Napoletana ("true Neapolitan pizza"), or VNP in Italy and worldwide. To be Vera Pizza Napoletana, pizza must be made according to the AVPN's regulations for obtaining a collective brand mark by a pizzeria that pays annual AVPN dues. It specifies rules around the type of flour, salt, tomatoes, cheese, olive oil, and yeast; pH and temperature of the water; pizza height and diameter; the *amounts* of ingredients; length of time mixing, rising, and cooking; and surface and dome temperatures.

That's too many rules for me. The funny thing is many Italians don't follow them either. Once, while doing a pizza class in London, I was prepping in the same room as a bunch of Italian pizza chefs in their restaurant. They were from Sardinia but had made pizza in Naples. Suddenly, they're adding this white substance to their dough, and I'm like, "Is that . . . lard?!"

It was vegetable shortening, though they said their recipe was based on one from a pizzeria in Naples that *uses* lard. "It's a big thing in Naples," they said. "Lots of places put lard in dough. It's a big secret." As I understand it, if you had a pizzeria that existed before the AVPN formed, you could do whatever you wanted and remain certified. This means you have rules, but then you have this diverse group of people making pizza in Naples that look dissimilar and use different ingredients.

Make pizza according to AVPN rules. Just don't tell anyone who isn't they're "wrong." I had a client in Buenos Aires, named Angeles Zeballos, making pizza in a wood-fired oven that wasn't from Naples. We used Argentinean flour and mozzarella, Italian tomatoes (not San Marzanos), natural leavening, and local toppings. She wanted to call her pizza "Neapolitan" and put a "Pizza Napoletana" sign out front. The pizzas were fantastic. Technically Neapolitan? No. Is she wrong for breaking the rules? No.

This is where I'm not into AVPN. I don't care what you do except when you preach dogma. That's why, to avoid confusion, I call this style Neapolitanish. It's the construction and shape used while cooking at high temp, similar to pizzerias in Naples, but it bucks the rules. Like me.

Dimpling

For this technique, imagine you're punching keyboard keys, creating tiny dimples in the dough's center. The dough becomes flat overall but doesn't completely de-gas. You still create nice crumb post-bake and a better crisp.

neapolitanish dough

Makes 7 (250-gram) dough balls

1,000 grams (8 cups) flour (90% strong bread flour and 10% whole-grain flour)
630 grams (2¾ cups) water, at room temperature (68°F/20°C to 72°F/22°C)
150 grams (¾ cup) starter (3 to 5 hours after feeding it at room temperature)
20 grams (2 tablespoons) extra-virgin olive oil
30 grams (2 tablespoons) sea salt

BAKER'S PERCENTAGES

100% flour
63% water
15% starter
2% extra-virgin olive oil
3% sea salt

C lose enough in look and feel to echo the Naples original, but without its rules and regulations. The Neapolitans will disown you, but, and I say this with love for my Italian cousins, let 'em.

1. Weigh out all the ingredients in separate containers, remove 10 grams (about 2 tablespoons) of water, and reserve it.

2. Put the flour in a large mixing bowl.

3. In another large mixing bowl, combine the remaining 620 grams (2 cups plus 10 tablespoons) of water and the starter and break up the starter by hand until it's a uniform consistency.

4. Using your hand, create a crater in the flour and pour the water and starter mixture in the center.

5. Begin mixing with your dominant hand, working your way in a clockwise motion from the center of the bowl to the rim. When the ball has just come together and the bowl is clean, add the olive oil and mix by hand a few more minutes. Cover the bowl with plastic wrap and rest at room temperature for 30 minutes.

6. Uncover the dough ball and begin mixing by hand. Add the reserved 10 grams of water and the salt and mix until just combined.

7. Transfer the dough ball to a lightly oiled container and cover with a lid or plastic wrap. Allow to rest for 5 hours, stretching the dough into itself about halfway.

8. Remove the dough ball and place on a lightly floured surface. Lightly flour your hands and, using a dough scraper and scale, portion the dough into 250-gram dough balls.

9. Form each into a tight ball by folding it in on itself, being careful to handle the balls quickly and gently so as not to transfer too much heat to them.

10. Place the dough balls on a lightly floured tray. Lightly flour the surface of the dough balls and cover with plastic wrap. Proof at room temperature for 12 to 18 hours, until the dough balls have doubled in size. Transfer the dough to the refrigerator and let them rest for up to 48 hours or until ready to use. It can last up to 5 days in the fridge.

the margherita

Makes 1 (11-inch/28-cm) pizza

1 (250-g) Neapolitanish dough ball (page 90)

56 grams (¼ cup) Basic Tomato Sauce (page 52)

6 basil leaves

40 grams (about 1½ ounces) fresh mozzarella

13 grams (about ½ ounce) Parmigiano-Reggiano, finely grated

15 grams (1 tablespoon) extra-virgin olive oil, in a squeeze bottle

So there's a story you hear about Queen Margherita, with the idea that this pizza looked like an Italian flag. Did the pizza come first? Did the flag come first? Did the queen come first? I mean, come on, no one really *knows* if this happened. People didn't write about food the same way then—they were happy to not be dying, or in a war or something—and unless some letter laying everything out explicitly is discovered, the truth is lost.

The origin story doesn't *matter*. What matters is that this is a perfect dish and that the combination of fresh mozzarella, tomato, basil, and olive oil was a catalyst that sparked pizza's global explosion. And it's this equation that makes something . . . pizza. Added to a bagel, it's a pizza bagel. To a burger? Pizza burger.

I like to make my Margherita a few different ways. Mozzarella first, then splotching sauce on top is great, but you can also put the sauce down first and grate Parm into the sauce before the mozzarella. I like olive oil drizzled before or sometimes after. That's the beauty—it's five simple toppings, but the balance, amounts, and order in which you add them are what makes a Margherita *your* Margherita.

1. Preheat your hacked oven (see page 265) to 550°F (288°C) or set your high-temperature oven to 850°F (454°C).

2. Stretch out the dough according to the Neapolitanish method (see page 38).

3. Using a 2-ounce (60-ml) ladle or a large spoon, spread the sauce evenly on the dough (or use the *spulacci* technique; see page 37), leaving 1 inch (2½ cm) around the dough's circumference for the crust.

4. Gently tear the basil and place it evenly onto the sauce.

5. Using your fingers, tear off quarter-sized chunks of mozzarella and top directly onto the pizza, leaving about ¾ inch (2 cm) between each piece. Dust with the Parmigiano-Reggiano and, using a squeeze bottle, drizzle with the olive oil.

6. Bake the pizza directly on the stones of your hacked home oven for about 5 minutes or until the crust is nicely browned, rotating halfway through. In your high-temp oven cook for about 2 minutes or until leopard-spotted, rotating halfway through. Cut into 6 slices and serve.

WHITE PIES

WHITE PIE PHILOSOPHY

So, pizza is dough, sauce, cheese. You can argue you don't need sauce to have pizza, but a pizzeria requires sauce. If you're going to call what you're making pizza, you need one pizza that's tomato, mozzarella, dough. Personally, I love white pizzas. Many of my most successful pizzas have been white. People think you need a "white sauce" if there isn't going to be tomato sauce. But that's vague. What's white sauce anyway?

There's cream, and a lot of things you can do to flavor cream. I've been putting cream on pizza forever, but I was inspired by the way Joe Beddia of Pizzeria Beddia makes his whipped flavored cream sauces while helping him during his cookbook party. Joe made this "spring cream" that was cream, garlic, basil,

and chives tossed in a Cuisinart. (If you don't know, the original Pizzeria Beddia was this tiny place in Philly's Fishtown neighborhood where Joe, the owner, basically did everything and used only the highest-quality ingredients.)

He held the button until it stiffened into whipped cream, then spread it on the uncooked dough. I was blown away. It was savory, bright, and fresh with a beautiful light green color—really cool. And for lower temp, longer bakes in a gas oven, it works great. It's easily spreadable (or squirtable) for great coverage, and the cheese melts into the cream. Terrific technique. So that's something I started doing because it works well for my low-temperature Thin & Crispy style. All credit to Joe.

Pizza

What Makes a Good White Pizza

I have four guidelines when creating a white pizza.

CHEESE COVERAGE

If you have skinny shreds of mozzarella, they'll melt fast. I recommend keeping cheese in its original ball and tearing pieces as needed. If the mozz is cold, you'll need a smaller piece. If it's room-temperature or warm, larger pieces. The speed the cheese melts will be determined by its thermal density. In general, for white pies, shredded mozz or small pieces close together are key for them to spread in the oven before the unexposed dough burns. If you put a pizza in the oven, there's a difference between the crust, which is thicker, and the thin dough in the middle, which turns black and burns quickly. If that happens, your day is ruined. So, good coverage.

MOISTURE

All toppings need to be considered—will they add or remove moisture? For instance, if you put raw mushrooms on a pizza, they'll release moisture. If it's a long bake, the moisture might release or steam off, but some will likely remain. I know you've had a pie soaked in mushroom water. Breadcrumbs *soak up* moisture. So adding them to sauce will stiffen it. Those are ends of the spectrum. Some cheeses have more moisture. That also contributes to a pizza's moisture level. If you use a moist ingredient, you want something to soak up moisture. Or vice versa depending on your pie's main characters. Back to those mushrooms. Why not roast them first to remove moisture and concentrate flavor, then offset that with cream sauce? You get the idea.

GOLDEN RIVERS

A good starting point for white pizza is the classic style you'll find in New York City. Totonno's with garlic, mozz, ricotta, Parmigiano, and olive oil always comes to mind. You could put those things on a pizza and it will taste good, but it will be a blanket of white—little textural variance, cheesy, and visually one-note. The thing to shoot for is what I call "golden rivers." The concept is to create islands of mozzarella and ricotta with golden rivers that form between them. The cheese melts and patches reach for each other but don't meet because pieces started far enough away. You get channels between the cheese, the olive oil and Parmigiano turn golden, and garlic is trapped underneath. It's spectacular. If the pieces are *too* far apart, that space between will dry and create big black bubbles. It's a fine line. Depending on the mozzarella size and oven temperature, the mozzarella will melt differently. The key is that before they completely melt into each other, the pizza is finished cooking and that space between them will be filled with the parm and the olive oil and create golden rivers running through islands of mozzarella.

MAIN CHARACTER

Two reasons I like white pies: my love for seasonal vegetables and my topping philosophy, which centers on a main character. Seasonal vegetables are my favorite main characters. When a fruit or vegetable is in season, celebrate that. Sometimes tomato sauce isn't the best thing to support the flavors of vegetables as main characters. For instance, asparagus screams white pie. So I make a white or red pie depending on the main character. Just remember, in America, you can get anything you want any time of the year. That doesn't mean it will be in season and delicious.

classic white pizza

Makes 1 (13-inch/33-cm) pizza

This could be one of the simplest and most difficult pizzas to pull off. Two things are key. The first? High-quality ingredients, especially the ricotta, but also mozzarella, garlic, olive oil, and Parm. The second is topping balance.

1 (250-g) Thin & Crispy dough ball (page 63)

2 cloves garlic, thinly sliced

55 grams (about 2 ounces) fresh mozzarella

28 grams (about 1 ounce) ricotta (fresh hand-dipped strongly recommended)

25 grams (about 1 ounce) Parmigiano-Reggiano, finely grated

10 grams (2 teaspoons) extra-virgin olive oil, in a squeeze bottle

Freshly ground black pepper

Pinch chile flakes

1. Preheat the oven with pizza stones to your oven's highest temperature setting (usually 550°F/288°C).

2. Stretch out the dough according to the Thin & Crispy method (see page 38).

3. Cover dough with the garlic, a piece every few inches, starting from the outside and working your way in.

4. Using your fingers, tear off quarter-sized chunks of mozzarella and top directly onto the pizza, leaving about ¾ inch (2 cm) between each piece.

5. Using a piping bag, squeeze small coin sized dollops of ricotta between pieces of mozzarella on the dough, starting from the outside in. There should be some room between the ricotta and mozzarella.

6. Dust with half of the Parmigiano-Reggiano. Carefully staying away from the outer 2 inches (5 cm) of the dough's edge, using a squeeze bottle, drizzle the pizza with the olive oil in a spiral starting from 2 inches (5 cm) from the edge toward the center.

7. Bake the pizza directly on the pizza stone for 5½ minutes, or until the crust is nicely browned, checking the bottom and rotating it halfway through for an evenly colored crust.

8. Finish with the remaining Parmigiano-Reggiano and some black pepper, cut the pizza into 6 slices, and top with the chile flakes.

brussels sprouts pizza

Makes 1 (11-inch/28-cm) pizza

I hated Brussels sprouts as a kid, but that's because the people making them didn't know how to cook them. You have to blast Brussels sprouts—whether it's a hot pan, a furnace-hot oven, or a high-temp pizza oven. Shred them thinly on the mandoline with salt and olive oil, then hit them with high heat and pull them when they're charred but crunchy. They sweeten beautifully.

The reason this pizza is so good is how the sprouts pair with *guanciale*. There's no substitute for guanciale. You won't get the same flavor from bacon or pancetta—those would be good, but they're different. And it needs to be cut into lardons. I like the way they crisp while the fat stays intact and the meat doesn't overcook. It looks nice and has good texture.

1 (250-g) Neapolitanish dough ball (page 90)

55 grams (about 2 ounces) fresh mozzarella

30 grams (about 1 ounce) Roasted Brussels Sprouts (page 220)

30 grams (about 1 ounce) guanciale

25 grams (about 1 ounce) Pecorino-Romano, grated

10 grams (2 teaspoons) extra-virgin olive oil, in a squeeze bottle

Zest of 1 lemon

Freshly ground black pepper

1. Preheat your hacked oven to 550°F (288°C) or set your high-temperature oven to 850°F (454°C).

2. Stretch out the dough according to the Neapolitanish method (see page 38).

3. Using your fingers, tear off quarter-sized chunks of mozzarella, and starting from the outside in, top directly onto the pizza, leaving about ¾ inch (2 cm) between each piece. Starting from the outside in, top with the roasted Brussels sprouts and guanciale.

4. Bake the pizza directly on the stones of your hacked home oven for about 5 minutes or until the crust is nicely browned, rotating halfway through. In your high-temp oven cook for about 2 minutes or until leopard-spotted, rotating halfway through.

5. Cut the pizza into 6 slices and top with the Pecorino-Romano. Using a squeeze bottle, drizzle the pizza with the olive oil in a spiral starting from the outside in. Finish with the lemon zest and some black pepper.

Pizza

HAND-DIPPED RICOTTA

VERSUS. . . NEVER MIND

There's good, delicious ricotta, and then there's garbage called ricotta. They're entirely different things. Frankly, in America, there are a lot of products called ricotta that aren't good.

Buying hand-dipped ricotta is one way to avoid dense, flat, gritty—I don't know what it's called, but it's not ricotta. Good hand-dipped ricotta is light. It's milky and fresh tasting with natural sweetness. On pizza it melts in the oven, whereas so-called ricottas dry and stay still.

As far as hand-dipped ricottas go, there's Calabro out of East Haven, Connecticut, Lioni Latticini in Jersey, and Narragansett Creamery in Providence, Rhode Island. But man, otherwise, buyer beware—great ricotta or don't bother. Pick another recipe. I don't care. It's not worth using crappy ricotta.

shrimp scampi pizza

Makes 1 (13-inch/33-cm) pizza

I was working with Uptown Social in Charleston, South Carolina, and I wanted the essence of shrimp scampi—garlic, white wine, lemon, and butter—as a pizza base. Given the part of the country, I knew the shrimp would be world-class, but I didn't realize *how good*. I'd marinated shrimp during testing, but when Chef Jonathan Kaldas saw my recipe he said to me, "Taste these before you marinate them."

He took shrimp we'd gotten that morning from a boat belonging to Tarvin Seafood (they'd just caught them), peeled it, deveined it, and put it on a tray—no oil, salt, or anything—then into the oven for one minute. It was some of the best shrimp I've ever had. Perfectly seasoned out of the water. Amazing.

Needless to say, there was no marinating the shrimp, and if you can get that kind of shrimp . . . don't marinate. Either way, the result is great. Everyone at the taste test agreed it was delicious—light and satisfying—but it didn't set the world on fire. It was too far from traditional ideas of pizza to hit nostalgia notes. Still, I always think it *should* be in the pantheon of greats.

1 (250-g) Thin & Crispy dough ball (page 63)

75 grams (about 3 ounces) White Wine Lemon Cream Sauce (page 202)

50 grams (about 2 ounces) Marinated Shrimp (page 217)

30 grams (about 1 ounce) Red Pickled Chiles (page 219)

15 grams (about ½ ounce) Sourdough Breadcrumbs (page 226)

5 grams (½ tablespoon) Fried Garlic Chips (see page 212)

1 scallion, thinly sliced

2 grams (about 1/10 ounce) flat-leaf parsley, finely chopped

1 lemon, zested

10 grams (2 teaspoons) extra-virgin olive oil, in a squeeze bottle

1. Preheat the oven with pizza stones to your oven's highest temperature setting (usually 550°F/288°C).

2. Stretch out the dough according to the Thin & Crispy method (page 38).

3. Using a 2-ounce (60-ml) ladle or a large spoon, spread the cream sauce evenly on the dough, leaving 1 inch (2½ cm) around the circumference for the crust.

4. Starting where the saucing begins and working from the outside in, lay down pieces of marinated shrimp every inch or so until they are evenly spaced and cover the dough. Place the pickled chiles between the shrimp and cover the pizza with breadcrumbs.

5. Bake the pizza directly on the pizza stone for 5½ minutes, or until the crust is nicely browned, checking the bottom and rotating it halfway through for an evenly colored crust.

6. Cut the pizza into 6 slices and top with the garlic chips, scallion, parsley, and lemon zest. Using a squeeze bottle, drizzle the pizza with olive oil in a spiral starting from the outside in.

Zen and the Art of Shrimp Pizza

Unless they are tiny, you never want whole shrimp on pizza.
You'll end up with one bite of pizza where you're wrangling
with a full shrimp and two other slices that have none at all.
Pieces the size of a medium coin, like a nickel, work great. They
distribute flavor and weigh down the dough if you're making a
cheeseless pie—a likely scenario if you're making a shrimp pie
because shrimp and cheese on pizza? Eh, not my favorite.

clam pizza

Makes 1 (11-inch/28-cm) pizza

---

50 grams (2 dozen) littleneck clams
1 lemon
56 grams (2 ounces/4 tablespoons) unsalted butter
1 medium (150 g) yellow onion, thinly sliced
1 large fennel bulb, thinly sliced
7 cloves (5 g) garlic, thinly sliced
3 sprigs thyme sprigs
3 dried bay leaves
240 grams (1 cup) white wine
120 grams (½ cup) heavy cream
1 (250-g) Neapolitanish dough ball (page 90)
25 grams (about 1 ounce) Sourdough Breadcrumbs (page 226)
Chile flakes, sliced scallions, chopped flat-leaf parsley, fennel fronds,
and lemon wedges for garnish

My client in Portugal, Lupita Pizzaria, is a favorite. It's a small place in Lisbon focused on quality and local ingredients, and its chef Duda Ferreira is super talented. We used a local stone-milled flour from just outside Lisbon and were next to Mercado da Ribeira, an old market by the waterfront, which meant access to wonderful fruit, vegetable, and spice stalls and a seafood market.

The seafood market is run by women. Apparently, the men are fishing. Duda knows the market and said there's a stall run by a woman named Rosa that's the best. He was right. She had a beautiful selection and a little sign that read, *O mar dá, a Rosa entrega*, which means, "The sea provides, and Rosa delivers." Great slogan. We bought fantastic little clams, collected aromatics—fennel, onion, garlic, scallions, thyme, and bay leaf—and made amazing clam pizza.

Get your aromatics going in a deep saucepan with butter, soft and sizzling, add clams just to the point of warming the outside of the shells, then turn the heat up and pour some nice white wine over everything. It should sizzle immediately. Trap that steam with a lid, give it a minute, and the clams will open. Pull them out, pluck them from the shells, ice them, and discard the shells. You're going to reduce the wine and clam liquor, strain it, add cream and reduce again, and you'll have an incredible sauce for your base.

Use thinly sliced fennel, onions, and breadcrumbs to weigh down the dough, top the sauce with clams, then out of the oven, dress the pie with lemon zest, lemon juice, fennel fronds, parsley, scallion, and breadcrumbs. It's amazing. If you can find anything *close* to what Rosa provided us, you'll really enjoy this pizza.

1. In a large bowl, cover the clams with cold water and let them sit for at least 30 minutes before cooking the pizza. Drain and rinse immediately before use. They can last in the fridge in water for a couple of days.

2. Using a vegetable peeler or paring knife, remove 3 large strips of lemon zest and set them aside. Juice the remaining lemon and reserve.

3. In a large heavy-bottomed pot, melt the butter over medium heat. Add the onions and fennel and cook until translucent, about 10 minutes. Add the garlic and continue to cook for an additional 2 minutes.

4. Add the thyme, bay leaves, and lemon peel. Adjust the heat to high and cook until the pan is sizzling.

5. Add the clams and continue to cook over high heat until the pan begins to sizzle again. Add the white wine, stir, and cover. Steam should release immediately after adding the wine.

6. After about 5 minutes, the clams will begin to open. Using a pair of tongs, carefully remove the clams as they open and set them aside. Discard any that do not open. Might take up to 15 minutes for clams to open depending on size of clam.

7. When the clams have been removed, strain the remaining liquid through a fine-mesh sieve. Gently push down on the solids and return the liquid to the pan. Adjust the heat to medium and reduce the liquid by half, or until syrupy. Slowly whisk in the cream and reduce by half. Add the reserved lemon juice, taste, and adjust the seasoning. Transfer the sauce to a metal or glass bowl, set over an ice bath, and chill immediately.

8. Meanwhile, shuck the clams and chill in a separate container.

9. To make the pizza, preheat your hacked oven (see page 265) to 550°F (288°C) or set your high-temperature oven to 850°F (454°C).

10. Stretch out the dough according to the Neapolitanish method (see page 38).

11. Using a 2-ounce (60-ml) ladle and starting from the outside in, top with the cream sauce.

12. Starting from the outside in, distribute the shucked clams evenly on the dough. Dust with the breadcrumbs.

13. Bake the pizza directly on the stones of your hacked home oven for about 5 minutes or until the crust is nicely browned, rotating halfway through. In your high-temp oven cook for about 2 minutes or until leopard-spotted, rotating halfway through.

14. Cut the pizza into 6 slices and finish with the chile flakes, scallions, parsley, fennel fronds, and a little lemon juice.

mushroom & onion pizza

Makes 1 (11-inch/28-cm) pizza

Remember, when topping white pies, it's important to cover the pizza completely because, without sauce, burnt dry spots will happen. Use any un-cheesed spaces on the dough for this recipe as the final flavor resting places of the roasted chanterelles.

1 (250-g) Neapolitanish dough ball (page 90)

55 grams (about 2 ounces) fresh mozzarella

20 grams (about ¾ ounce) Bayley Hazen Blue (or Gorgonzola), crumbled

30 grams (about 1 ounce) Oven-Roasted Fancy Mixed Mushrooms (page 220; use chanterelles and roast in one pan)

20 grams (about ¾ ounce) red onion, thinly sliced

Zest of 1 lemon (about 1 tablespoon)

Freshly ground black pepper

1. Preheat your hacked oven (see page 265) to 550°F (288°C) or set your high-temperature oven to 850°F (454°C).

2. Stretch out the dough according to the Neapolitanish method (see page 38).

3. Using your fingers, tear off quarter-sized chunks of mozzarella and, starting from the outside in, top directly onto the pizza, leaving about ¾ inch (2 cm) between each piece.

4. Place crumbles of blue cheese among the mozzarella chunks. Use the remaining empty spaces to place the chanterelles. Top with the sliced onions.

5. Bake the pizza directly on the stones of your hacked home oven for about 5 minutes or until the crust is nicely browned, rotating halfway through. In your high-temp oven cook for about 2 minutes or until leopard-spotted, rotating halfway through.

6. Cut the pizza into 6 slices and top with the lemon zest and some black pepper.

PAN PIZZAS

GRANDMA PIZZAS

In New York City, the term *grandma pie* signifies a certain kind of pizza. Depending on which origin story you believe or who makes your favorite "grandma slice," it can mean different things in terms of slice *height* or proofing times.

Exact thickness doesn't matter. Shape doesn't matter. What kind of pan? Whatever shape pan you have. Whatever shape pan your grandma has.

Grandma pizza is in the spectrum of Sicilian pizza, just like Detroit-style pizza is. To me, these pan pizzas are all in the category of Sicilian Grandma. A pizza brought to America by Sicilians, and grandmas.

pizza

sicilian grandma dough

Makes 2 (900-gram) Sicilian pizzas or 3 (700-gram) grandma pizzas

900 grams high-protein flour
100 grams whole-grain flour, preferably freshly milled
30 grams sea salt
720 grams (3 cups) water, at 65°F (18°C)
100 grams starter (3 to 5 hours after feeding it at room temperature)
60 grams extra-virgin olive oil, plus more for oiling the pans

BAKER'S PERCENTAGES

100% flour
72% water
10% starter
6% extra-virgin olive oil
3% sea salt

This recipe is based on memory but a strong one: a dark brown chewy crust, a thick sauce, olives, onions, mushrooms, and dried oregano. It was oily but there was no cheese. The main thing was the way the toppings thickened the sauce. I still love veggie-heavy pizzas—the basis for my belief that good olives are always great on pizza.

Unfortunately, Great-Grandma Lena isn't around to share her recipe. Even if she was, I doubt I'd get more than "a pinch of this, a pinch of that." So, I've taken a technical approach to recreating something ephemeral. Why? It's my first pizza memory. You can use this recipe for either grandma pies or thicker-crusted New York City–style Sicilian pizzas. Portion the dough into smaller 700-gram balls for Grandma and 900-gram balls for Sicilian. Play around with pan and gram sizes to see what works best for you. See page 30 for pan recommendations.

1. Weigh all the ingredients in separate containers. In a large mixing bowl, combine the flours and salt and mix thoroughly with clean hands.

2. In another large mixing bowl, combine the water and starter.

3. Create a crater in the flour and pour the liquids in the center.

4. Begin mixing with your dominant hand. Start in the center of the bowl and mix in a clockwise fashion until the dough comes together, at this point add 60 grams of olive oil and continue to mix until the dough is fully incorporated. Stop mixing, cover the bowl with plastic wrap, and set aside for 30 to 45 minutes.

5. Mix by stretching and folding the dough onto itself for about 6 minutes.

6. Transfer the dough to a lightly oiled container with a lid (or a bowl tightly covered with plastic wrap) and let it rest at room temperature. Stretch and fold the dough for 1 minute every 30 minutes for 3 hours (six times).

7. Rest at room temperature (covered) for 30 minutes.

8. Using about 40 grams of olive oil, lightly oil two or three baking pans.

9. Lightly flour your hands, and using a dough cutter and scale, portion then shape the dough (three 700-gram or two 900-gram pieces) into rectangles by folding the edges into themselves.

10. Transfer each dough to the center of a pre-oiled baking pan. Cover each pan with plastic wrap and allow to rest at room temperature for 1 hour.

11. Lift the dough and press out any air from the bottom of the pan. Carefully stretch the dough to the pan's edges. Using your fingertips, gently dimple the entire length of the dough. Cover and let proof at room temperature for 6-12 hours or until the dough has doubled in size.

12. Par-bake or top and bake according to your chosen recipe's instructions. Just add 10 minutes to the bake time if you skip the par-bake.

Pizza

How to Go Viral

I'm kidding—you can't plan to go viral. Well, you can position yourself to have the potential to get attention, but you can't command the Internet gods (and you don't want to tempt them). Anyway, here's an example of how something in the pizza world takes off.

My ButterCrust recipe came about because I was recreating the '80s-style Pizza Hut Pan Pizza for a "Hot Ones" video for First We Feast with Andrew W.K. and Sean Evans (it's on YouTube). Andrew called it "the best pizza he's eaten in his life," so I guess I did something right.

First, I put myself in a place where that video was going to happen, right? Then I posted about the recipe as I tested it on Instagram. Another avenue for the universe to run with it. Then I gave it an appealing name: "ButterCrust Pan Pizza." I mean, what was I going to call it, "Pizza Hut Pan Pizza"? Don't you want to eat something called ButterCrust Pan Pizza?

People freaked. Then Sam Sifton, *New York Times* food impresario, came across it and messaged, "What is this ButterCrust recipe?" I gave him the recipe, the *New York Times* published it with the suggestion of using a skillet, and boom. Internet-famous for butter pizza.

new york–style grandma pizza

Makes 1 (12-by-16-inch/30-by-40-cm) pan pizza

This is the grandma pizza you encounter in New York. It's just an adaptation of a pizza that existed everywhere in Sicilian homes, whether it be in Chicago, New York City, Texas, or Sicily. It's grandma pizza. And you can make it in your home even if you're not Sicilian or a grandma.

1 half sheet pan (700 g)
Sicilian Grandma dough (page 116),
proofed and ready to top

180 grams (about 6 ounces)
low-moisture mozzarella, shredded

110 grams (about 4 ounces)
fresh mozzarella

Pinch dried wild Sicilian oregano,
stems removed

102 grams (½ cup) Spicy Grandma
Sauce (page 56)

20 grams (5) Sicilian anchovy fillets,
deboned and chopped into small pieces
(optional)

25 grams (about 1 ounce)
Pecorino-Romano, finely grated

30 grams (2 tablespoons)
extra-virgin olive oil, in a squeeze bottle

1. Preheat the oven with pizza stones to 475°F (250°C).

2. Top the pizza with the low-moisture mozzarella. Go all the way to the edge.

3. Using your fingers, pinch off coin sized pieces of fresh mozzarella and evenly disperse onto the pizza. Dust with the oregano.

4. Using a 2-ounce (60-ml) ladle or a large spoon, spread the spicy tomato sauce using the *spulacci* technique (see page 37). Add the anchovies evenly starting from the outside in.

5. Bake the pizza directly on the pizza stone for 15 to 20 minutes, until the crust is golden brown.

6. Remove the pizza from the pan with an offset spatula and transfer to a cooling rack. Top with the Pecorino and, using a squeeze bottle, drizzle with the olive oil. Allow to cool for 5 minutes before cutting.

Pizza

onion AND olive bread

Makes 1 (12-by-16-inch/30-by-40-cm) pan pizza

---

15 grams (about ½ ounce) green **Castelvetrano olives**, pitted and sliced
20 grams (about ¾ ounce) black olives, pitted and sliced
20 grams (about ¾ ounce) red onion, thinly sliced
12˝ round pan or 1 half sheet pan (**900 g**) **Sicilian Grandma dough** (page 116)
40 grams (3 tablespoons) extra-virgin olive oil
Large flake or coarse sea salt for garnish

I had incredible Italian Taggiasca olives in Kuwait (the chef I worked with was from Northern Italy, where the olives are sourced). Sicilians love their green Castelvetrano olives. I could go on. Here's what to remember: Whichever olive you choose will be the main character of this pizza, but most any will work because they're paired with the sweetness of onions. Both the onions and the olives sink into the dough, which will be light and fluffy in places and dense and chewy where the moisture of the olives and onions is trapped. This is a nostalgic pizza for me. It could become one for you.

1. Spread the olives and red onion onto the dough and very gently press until they sink into the dough. Drizzle the olive oil on the whole pizza and sprinkle with a few pinches of salt. Cover with plastic wrap or a lid and allow the dough to proof for about 3 hours at room temperature.

2. Once the dough has risen around the olives and onions, preheat the oven with pizza stones to 475°F (250°C).

3. Remove the cover, put the pan in the oven directly on the stone, and bake for 15 to 20 minutes, until the crust is golden brown.

4. Remove the pizza from the pan with an offset spatula and transfer to a cooling rack. Allow to cool for 5 minutes before cutting.

garlic, caramelized onion, anchovy AND breadcrumb sicilian pizza

Makes 1 (12-by-16-inch/30-by-40-cm) pan pizza

12″ round pan or 1 half sheet pan (900 g) Sicilian Grandma dough (page 116), proofed and ready to top
168 grams (¾ cup) Basic Tomato Sauce (see page 52)
20 grams (5) Sicilian anchovy fillets, deboned and chopped into small pieces
50 grams (about 1¾ ounces) Sourdough Breadcrumbs (page 226)
30 grams (about 1 ounce) caciocavallo, shredded
25 grams (about 1 ounce) Pecorino-Romano, finely grated
40 grams (3 tablespoons) extra-virgin olive oil, in a squeeze bottle
60 grams (about 2 ounces) Caramelized Onions (page 209)

This is something my dad grew up eating that was around when I was a kid but that I didn't eat because we were vegetarians. It was only later I finally had it, but when I did . . .

1. Preheat the oven with pizza stones to 475°F (250°C).

2. Using the back of a large spoon or ladle, spread the tomato sauce in an even layer over the dough.

3. Evenly top the pizza with the anchovies. Dust with the breadcrumbs. The breadcrumbs should soak into the sauce—there shouldn't be any patches of dry breadcrumbs.

4. Top the pizza with all of the caciocavallo and half of the Pecorino. Using a squeeze bottle, drizzle with the olive oil then evenly top the pizza with the caramelized onions.

5. Remove the pizza from the pan with an offset spatula and transfer to a cooling rack. Allow to cool for 5 minutes before cutting into 8 slices, then cover the pizza with the remaining Pecorino.

classic upside-down sicilian

Makes 1 (12-by-16-inch/30-by-40-cm) pan pizza

**1 half sheet pan (900 g) Sicilian Grandma dough (page 116),
proofed and ready to top**
250 grams (about 9 ounces) low-moisture mozzarella, thinly sliced
102 grams (½ cup) Basic Tomato Sauce (page 52)
25 grams (about 1 ounce) Sourdough Breadcrumbs (page 226)
50 grams (about 1¾ ounces) Pecorino-Romano, finely grated
40 grams (3 tablespoons) extra-virgin olive oil, in a squeeze bottle
2 pinches dried wild Sicilian oregano, stems removed

The Sicilian slice can be found all over New York City. This is a variation where you see the mozzarella layered first, then sauce, cooked down and split off, creating cracks and cheese crevices. You get this creamy, melty layer of mozzarella underneath, and gummy dough where it comes together with the cheese. It's a little raw but in a good way, and there's a big, fluffy crust underneath with a crispy bottom. You get a hint of oregano and a sprinkling of Pecorino. That's it. And the cheese doesn't slide off because it's adhered to the dough. Done right, it's a special New York slice.

1. Preheat the oven with pizza stones to 475°F (250°C).

2. Cover the dough with the mozzarella in a single layer. Using a 2-ounce (60-ml) ladle, completely cover the mozzarella with the tomato sauce. Sprinkle the breadcrumbs and half of the Pecorino evenly across the sauce. Using a squeeze bottle, drizzle with the olive oil.

3. Bake the pizza in its pan directly on the pizza stone for 15 to 20 minutes, until the crust is golden brown and the cheese has begun to brown.

4. Remove the pizza from the pan with an offset spatula and transfer to a cooling rack. Top with the remaining Pecorino and the oregano. Allow to cool for 5 minutes before cutting into 8 slices.

spicy pepperoni sicilian pizza

Makes 1 (12-by-16-inch/30-by-40-cm) pan pizza

---

1 half sheet pan (900 g) Sicilian Grandma dough (see page 116),
proofed and ready to top
250 grams (about 9 ounces) low-moisture mozzarella, thinly sliced
102 grams (½ cup) Spicy Grandma Sauce (page 56)
50 grams (about 1¾ ounces) Parmigiano-Reggiano cheese, finely grated
2 pinches dried wild Sicilian oregano, stems removed
60 grams (about 2 ounces) pepperoni, sliced (about 25 pieces)
40 grams (3 tablespoons) extra-virgin olive oil, in a squeeze bottle

Everyone loves a spicy pepperoni pizza, and a spicy Sicilian pepperoni pan pizza is its highest form. I've addressed why making pepperoni pizza spicier is a great idea--especially if you use fresh chiles and chile flakes, and we use both in the spicy grandma sauce.

1. Preheat the oven with pizza stones to 475°F (250°C).

2. Cover the dough with the mozzarella in a single layer. Using a 2-ounce (60-ml) ladle, completely cover the mozzarella with the tomato sauce.

3. Spread half of the Parmigiano-Reggiano evenly over the sauce and sprinkle with the oregano. Place the pepperoni evenly on the pizza, starting from the outside in. Remember: Pepperoni migration is unavoidable! Don't be surprised if the slices aren't where you left them. Using a squeeze bottle, drizzle with the olive oil.

4. Bake the pizza in its pan directly on the pizza stone for 15 to 20 minutes, until the crust is golden brown and the cheese has begun to brown.

5. Remove the pizza from the pan with an offset spatula and transfer to a cooling rack. Top with the remaining Parmigiano-Reggiano. Allow to cool for 5 minutes before cutting into 8 slices.

faccia di vecchia (old lady's face pizza)

Makes 1 (12-by-16-inch/30-by-40-cm) pan pizza

I'm in the town of Cammarata, touring west-central Sicily, and my guide is this local, Enzo, a sweet guy and a big character. Sicily's full of big characters, and by big, I don't mean tall. Enzo is introducing us to people, we're walking with the town's vice mayor, and we have a translator. Enzo and the vice mayor respond to the translator in Italian but occasionally break off into Sicilian dialect. Enzo knows about my Sicilian heritage. He's testing me.

The dialect wasn't passed to my dad—that generation wanted to be cowboys—but I grew up hearing my great-grandmother use it. I learned a few words, mostly insults. There's *gagootz*, a Sicilian way to say *cacuzza*, a giant squash, and also a way to say someone's not very smart. Enzo asked, "What'd they call pizza?" I was like, "Well, now that you mention it, my dad always said my great-grandmother never said *pizza*. She called it *faccia di vecchia*. But I never heard anybody else say it."

That excites Enzo ("Yeah, that's our signature dish!") and we're having this conversation while walking down this narrow street a tiny car is navigating—inches on either side. We're huddling in a doorway so it can pass, which it does then stops. Enzo knows the guy, they talk, the guy gets out, pops his trunk, and it's full of . . . *faccia di vecchia*. It's fresh from the bakery on the way to be sold. He gives me one and refuses money. Enzo says, "This is it! *Faccia di vecchia*."

It was similar to what I grew up eating. We tore off pieces and walked the streets snacking and it was like, "This is it! I'm in the right place in the universe at the right time." And now you can make it at home and have your own small-town Sicilian experience.

100 grams (about 3½ ounces) Sicilian Onion Topping (page 229)
1 half sheet pan (700 g) Sicilian Grandma dough (page 116), proofed and ready to top
30 grams (about 1 ounce) caciocavallo, shredded
25 grams (about 1 ounce) Pecorino-Romano, finely grated
20 grams (1½ tablespoons) extra-virgin olive oil, in a squeeze bottle

1. Preheat the oven with pizza stones to 475°F (250°C).

2. Spread the Sicilian onion topping onto the entire pizza, leaving about ½ inch (12 mm) around the dough's circumference for the crust.

3. Top the pizza with the caciocavallo and half of the Pecorino.

4. Bake the pizza directly on the pizza stone for 15 to 20 minutes, until the crust is golden brown and the cheese has begun to brown.

5. Remove the pizza from pan with an offset spatula and transfer to a cooling rack. Top with the remaining Pecorino and, using a squeeze bottle, drizzle with the olive oil. Allow to cool for 5 minutes before cutting into 8 slices.

BUTTERCRUST PAN PIZZA

Where do grandma pizzas end and pan pizzas begin? An eternal question. You know it when you see it. I'd never consider Pizza Hut–type pan pizzas (as much as I loved them as a kid) grandma pizzas.

Growing up in Austin, Texas, there was a bakery in nearby San Antonio called Butter-Krust. The company donated textbook covers to our school, and certain classes (not mine, tragically) got a factory tour. We showed our gratitude as a student body by modifying these covers to read, "Butt Krust." I remember this every time I recreate the buttery crust signature to Pizza Hut's pan pizzas of the '80s, my childhood pizza.

I grew up eating world-class pizza in Texas. Falcos emigrated from Sicily at the turn of the century when multiple villages in the Belice Valley (in southwestern Sicily) unloaded truckloads of peasants in central Texas (of all places). They were invited to work "The Bottom," the flood-prone farmland along the Brazos River.

My Sicilian great-grandmother spent her life gardening and cooking for her family. Her pizza was the first I ever had—super legit Sicilian grandma pies. I liked her pizza. But as I've admitted, what I *loved* was Pizza Hut's personal pan pizza. Buttery crust, sweet sauce, and all the stringy chewy mozzarella that could be physically packed on a pizza. Being the little shithead that I was, I'd tell my great-grandma to her face, "I don't want your pizza, Great-Grandma. I want Pizza Hut!"

I wish I could go back in time and punch that kid in the face. But after assailing my six-year-old self, my next stop would be Pizza Hut because it was good—you're not imagining it. After decades of corporate buyouts and an ingredients race to the bottom for profits, those personal pan pizzas of your childhood BOOK IT! Program days (Remember that reading program they had that rewarded children with free pizza?) are gone forever. Except now I have a better recipe.

Behold, the 1980s-era buttercrust pan pizza!

buttercrust pan pizza dough

Makes 3 (12-inch/30-cm diameter) round pan pizza doughs

Note: Will make about 5 personal pan pizzas if using a 9-inch round pizza pan with 350-gram dough ball.

1,000 grams high-protein bread flour
30 grams sea salt
650 grams water, at room temperature (68°F to 72°F/20°C to 22°C)
100 grams starter (3 to 5 hours after feeding it at room temperature)
5 grams cake or fresh yeast (or 1.58 grams instant yeast)
230 grams unsalted butter

BAKER'S PERCENTAGES

Flour 100%

Water 65%

Starter 10%

Butter 10%

Salt 3%

Commercial Yeast 0.5%

When I think of Pizza Hut Pan Pizza, I think of butter. In the Midwest, they do deep-dish with butter that's more like a piecrust. This one . . . the crust is more delicate. Toppings feel a little precariously weighty on the dough, but it stays intact, and when everything times up right, it has this brioche-soft texture that's not chewy at all. It's buttery and delicious—a naughty pizza in the best possible way.

1. Weigh out each ingredient in separate containers.

2. Cube and refrigerate 60 grams of the butter. Melt 40 grams of the butter and set aside. Allow the remaining 130 grams of butter to come to room temperature.

3. In a large mixing bowl, combine the flour and salt. Using clean hands, mix thoroughly.

4. In another large mixing bowl, combine the water, starter, fresh yeast, and melted butter. Mix by hand, making sure to break up any large pieces.

5. Create a crater in the flour and pour the liquids in the center. Begin mixing with just your dominant hand until the dough lifts from the sides of the bowl and forms a ball. Stop mixing, cover with plastic wrap, and rest for 30 minutes at room temperature.

6. Remove the chilled butter from the refrigerator. Gradually add it to the rested dough and combine by gently stretching and folding. Continue for 10 minutes, then transfer to a lightly oiled container. Cover with plastic wrap and rest for 3 hours at room temperature.

7. Using the 130 grams room temperature butter, grease 3 (12-inch/30-cm diameter) round deep-dish pans and set aside.

8. Divide the dough into thirds, 650 grams each, and shape each into a ball by folding it in on itself. Transfer the dough to the buttered pans. Cover each pan with plastic wrap and allow to rest at room temperature for 3 hours.

9. Lift the dough and press out any air from the bottom of the pan. Using your fingertips, gently dimple the entire length of the dough. Cover and proof for another 3 hours, then transfer to the refrigerator and leave overnight or up to 18 hours.

10. Remove the dough and allow it to reach room temperature for 3 to 5 hours before baking.

11. To par-bake, preheat the oven with pizza stones to 475°F (250°C).

12. Remove the cover and par-bake the un-topped dough for 10 minutes.

   Note: Sometimes I par-bake, sometimes I don't. I like both methods, so you should try each method for yourself. Just add 10 minutes to the bake time if you skip the par-bake.

cheesy pan pizza

Makes 1 (12-inch/30-cm diameter) round pan pizza

1 12-inch/30-cm round pan (650 g) ButterCrust dough, par-baked and ready to top
(page 136)

102 grams (½ cup) Robust Tomato Sauce (page 54)

Pinch dried wild Sicilian oregano, stems removed

Pinch dried Calabrian chile flakes

25 grams (about 1 ounce) Parmigiano-Reggiano, finely grated

25 grams (about 1 ounce) Pecorino-Romano, finely grated

60 grams (about 2 ounces) fresh mozzarella

230 grams (about 8 ounces) low-moisture part-skim mozzarella, shredded

115 grams (about 4 ounces) low-moisture whole milk mozzarella, shredded

One of the keys to making a great pan cheese pizza is . . . cheese! Way more than you'd think. And *good* cheese. You've got all this dough because it's a pan pie, and because you have so much dough, you want a ton of cheese. You get this pool of molten cheese that's brown and crusty but liquid and stretchy underneath. The other thing is simplicity. A little more of a seasoned sauce because there are no toppings—some spice, maybe garlic, oregano, and Parmigiano-Reggiano. That's it.

1. Preheat the oven with pizza stones to 475°F (250°C).

2. Immediately after taking the par-baked pizza out of the oven, using a 2-ounce (60-ml) ladle or a large spoon, spread the tomato sauce onto the entire pizza, leaving about ½ inch (12 mm) around the dough's edge for the crust. Dust with the oregano, chile flakes, Parmigiano-Reggiano, and Pecorino.

3. Evenly distribute the fresh mozzarella, then both shredded mozzarellas, and transfer to the oven.

4. Put the pan in the oven directly on the pizza stone and bake for 15 to 20 minutes, or until the crust and cheese are golden brown. The time will vary depending on your oven.

5. Remove the pizza from the pan with an offset spatula and transfer to a cooling rack. Allow to cool for 5 minutes before cutting into 8 slices.

veggie lover's pan pizza

Makes 1 (12-inch/30-cm diameter) round pan pizza

---

1 12-inch/30-cm round pan (650 g) ButterCrust dough, par-baked and ready to top (page 136)
56 grams (¼ cup) Robust Tomato Sauce (page 54)
25 grams (about 1 ounce) Parmigiano-Reggiano, finely grated
20 grams (about ¾ ounce) Pecorino-Romano, finely grated
Pinch dried wild Sicilian oregano, stems removed
225 grams (about 8 ounces) low-moisture part-skim mozzarella, shredded
115 grams (about 4 ounces) low-moisture whole milk mozzarella, shredded
60 grams (about 2 ounces) fresh mozzarella
20 grams (about ¾ ounce) green bell pepper, julienned
25 grams (about 1 ounce) Oven-Roasted Fancy Mixed Mushrooms (page 220)
20 grams (about ¾ ounce) red onion, thinly sliced
20 grams (about ¾ ounce) black olives, pitted and quartered
15 grams (1 tablespoon) white balsamic vinegar

When I was growing up vegetarian, this was our go-to order at the Brick Oven, one of the pizzerias we'd frequent as a family in Austin. Their Veggie Lover's Pizza had mushrooms, olives, onions, green peppers, mozzarella, and tomato. There's the sour of the olives, the sweetness of the onions, the crunchiness of the peppers, and umami from the mushrooms. I love this pie. But those diced raw tomatoes—they drove me crazy. No thanks. *Mayyybee* in tomato season, but even then, I don't want crappy "fresh" tomatoes.

1. Preheat the oven with pizza stones to 475°F (250°C).

2. Immediately after taking the par-baked pizza out of the oven, using a 2-ounce (60-ml) ladle or a large spoon, spread the tomato sauce onto the entire pizza, leaving about ½ inch (12 mm) around the dough's edge for the crust.

3. Top the sauce with the grated cheeses. Pinch the oregano onto the sauce and cheese. Follow with the fresh mozzarella and then both shredded mozzarellas. Finish with the bell pepper, mushrooms, onion, and olives.

4. Put the pan in the oven directly on the pizza stone and bake for 15 to 20 minutes, or until the crust and cheese are golden brown. The time will vary depending on your oven.

5. Remove the pizza from the pan with an offset spatula and transfer to a cooling rack. Drizzle the whole pie with the vinegar. Allow to cool for 5 minutes before cutting into 8 slices.

supreme pan pizza

Makes 1 (12-inch/30-cm diameter)
round pan pizza

**1 12-inch/30-cm round pan (650 g)
ButterCrust dough, par-baked and
ready to top (page 136)**

**112 grams (½ cup) Robust Tomato
Sauce (page 54)**

**60 grams (about 2 ounces)
fresh mozzarella**

**225 grams (about 8 ounces)
low-moisture whole milk mozzarella,
shredded**

**25 grams (about 1 ounce)
Parmigiano-Reggiano, finely grated**

**20 grams (about ¾ ounce)
green bell pepper, julienned**

**20 grams (about ¾ ounce) red onion,
thinly sliced**

**20 grams (about ¾ ounce) black olives,
pitted and quartered**

**50 grams (6 slices)
Salumeria Biellese pepperoni (or
similar large-diameter pepperoni)**

**60 grams (about 2 ounces)
Falco Sausage (page 211)**

**25 grams (about 1 ounce)
Pecorino-Romano, finely grated**

**Pinch dried wild Sicilian oregano,
stems removed**

What makes a pizza supreme? A combination of toppings from Veggie Lover's and Meat Lover's pies—more than one meat and at least one veggie. The most classic Supreme is sausage, pepperoni, bell peppers, onions, mushrooms, and olives. I think you need to pull back a bit so it's not overloaded. I do sausage, pepperoni, onions, olives, and peppers. But a Supreme still has to be somewhat supreme! I do a version at General Assembly in Toronto called the Supreme Leader with tomato, aged mozzarella, Pecorino, pepperoni, homemade pork sausage, double-smoked bacon, and jalapeño. It's . . . supreme.

1. Preheat the oven with pizza stones to 475°F (250°C).

2. Immediately after taking the par-baked pizza out of the oven, using a 2-ounce (60-ml) ladle or large spoon, spread the tomato sauce onto the entire pizza, leaving about ½ inch (12 mm) around the dough's edge for the crust. Top the sauce with the mozzarella (fresh, then shredded) and Parmigiano-Reggiano.

3. Add the peppers, onions, olives, and pepperoni. Using your fingers, pluck nickel-sized balls of sausage and distribute them evenly on the pizza.

4. Put the pan in the oven directly on the stone and bake for 20 to 25 minutes, or until the crust and cheese are golden brown. The time will vary depending on your oven.

5. Remove the pizza from the pan with an offset spatula and transfer to a cooling rack. Top with the Pecorino and dust with the oregano. Let cool for 5 minutes before cutting into 8 slices and serving.

INTERNATIONAL CONSULTING: TRAVEL

PICKING AND LAUNCHING PROJECTS

I don't do a lot of improvements to existing pizzerias. I specialize in new projects. My expertise is in designing kitchens, workflow, and brand building—things that are interconnected. It's important to be involved in all of that. So projects usually start with a client approaching me with an idea. What kind of clients? How long do projects take? How do we arrive at different styles and menus? How do you build a team? Come into my office.

I want every project I work on to be a long-term success and one of the top pizza places in whatever city, state, or country it's in. So I prefer to work with clients who have restaurant experience (whether as a chef, front-of-house server, sommelier, operator, or builder). You need *some* connection and understanding because this is not for everyone and it's difficult to try to help someone who suddenly realizes they're in the wrong business. I don't take clients who think opening a pizzeria will be easy or that they'll just do it on the side. Come to me because you *know* you want to do this and want to do it the best way.

Project Length

It's very rare that I jump into a place preparing to open and we're done in under a year. Design, building, permitting, hiring . . . a lot of things must happen before dough gets stretched. Some projects take two years before we make a pizza.

How to Pick a Pizza Style?

Clients usually have an idea of what they want to do. That's good. Come to me for expertise, not inspiration. My client Rohit in Thailand went to NYU and wanted to open a New York City–style slice shop in Bangkok. Great. Let's do it. And we did—it's called Soho Pizza and it's fantastic.

How Do Pies Come to Be?

It starts with dough and testing. My process is simple. We begin with the baseline, cheese pizza. That involves decisions: dough, dough methodology, flour, oven, oven temperature, and the pan (if it's a pan pie). Now . . . sauce. You have to pick the tomato. How will the sauce be cooked (*if* it will be cooked). And cheese. Fresh or aged? Will you stretch mozzarella or buy it? Internationally, are we using local, Italian, or American ingredients? That's a lot of decisions before we've even made pizza. You may have the best idea in the history of pizza for a signature pie, but it's important not to complicate things at the beginning. Once you love the baseline, *then* you play.

Creating a Team

This is an ongoing process that involves every other aspect of the project. Understanding decisions, compartmentalizing them and problems that must be solved, watching how I work, getting clients involved in the physical work—a lot must happen. I don't just tell people what to do. I explain decisions I've made and recount my mistakes. This usually means long hours—fourteen-hour days. We clean, prep, do dishes, cook—together. *That's* how you create a team. That's how you lead.

Ensuring Consistency Post-Falco

I'm never really *gone*. I'm there for clients long after I'm not in the kitchen, whether that means panicked texts about dough, emails about new ingredients, or calls to celebrate reviews. But I can't be everywhere, so ensuring consistency is something I talk a lot about before, during, and after. But methodology is consistency's fail-safe. So I educate and instill all projects with processes that ensure results in perpetuity. Cleanliness, consistency, and great ingredients—my three principles of pizza.

THE THREE PRINCIPLES

CLEANLINESS

This is number one—the result of having an organized kitchen and an organized mind.

CONSISTENCY

The result of a culture of integrity. It's about holding yourself and your product to the highest standard.

GREAT INGREDIENTS

It's all about community, knowing who you're sourcing from, a well-developed palate, and knowing what you want.

NEW YORK CITY

It's not the water.

That's the first thing people ask when it comes to the "secret" of New York City pizza.

But before we go further, the first thing I let them know is there's not that much great pizza in New York City.

I know. Sacrilege. But listen. Forget about it being the "birthplace of pizza in America." Which, by the way, is debatable. New York City is known for pizza because of the sheer number of pizzerias. But if you look at the *number* of pizzerias versus the amount of *great* pizza . . . eh. Collectively, New York City isn't doing great.

In addition to places losing the connection to their founders and shortcutting time-honored techniques, for decades corporations have tried swapping base ingredients for cheaper products. A lot of pizzerias that were small or owned by Italian-Americans and serviced immigrant communities making the pizza New York City built its reputation on grew into behemoths or have been acquired by corporations. When you're acquired, they cut costs. It's had a huge effect on the restaurant industry (and pizza) because there's this line between making something delicious and making money.

The New York City slice *became* the New York City slice because it was quick, cheap, and tasty. But at some point, the

cheap part became the priority and the tasty part was sacrificed.

Back to the water. If New York City tap water were magic, there wouldn't be shitty pizza. (There is.) *Is* the water good? Yeah. Our tap water's fantastic. Some of America's best. I love the way it tastes, and it's relatively pure compared to water in the rest of the country. It has low amounts of total dissolved solids, in the 20 to 30 parts per million range, and from what I've tested, there's little chlorine and the pH is usually between 6.5 and 7. As in Naples, New York City water is supplied by aqueducts from nearby mountain ranges (one built by the Romans millennia ago, the other at the turn of the twentieth century). The tap water in Los Angeles has a chlorine presence and total dissolved solids in the 300 to 400 parts per million range. That's a big difference! I've tried the water in both of these US cities—one tastes good and has less stuff in it, the other tastes bad and has more.

All of that said, there are great pizzerias in New York City, and more will always be opening. It's a style worth celebrating.

HOW TO JUDGE A
NEW YORK
SLICE

The hardest part of making good pizza is the dough. Most people who judge pizza don't know what to look for. You can impress an amateur palate with good sauce and cheese on mediocre dough.

In America, Bianco di Napoli tomatoes are amazing. So too Stanislaus California tomatoes. Even the cheapest places use Stanislaus (they have premium and pedestrian lines), so rarely are tomatoes problematic (or sauce by extension unless it's doctored with too much sugar, salt, pepper, spices, or herbs).

Similar with cheese. Most places use Grande. Some use Polly-O. There are smaller producers, like Pecoraro Cheese in Brooklyn (great) and BelGioioso Cheese (who I've partnered with in the past, and whose cheese is fantastic). But even places using cheaper mozzarella still use "real" cheese.

Here's what to do. Tear off the end of the crust, smell it, and taste it. If it doesn't taste or smell like much, like an underseasoned, bleached white bread that lacks characteristics of living wheat—no good. If there's crumb and the flavor of great seasoned bread, now we can talk.

TORONTO

After New York City, it's a tie between Toronto and São Paulo for where I've made the most pizza. Toronto is odd man out in that it's not a historic pizza city. There are small Italian communities and a Little Italy, but in my experience, Torontonians don't talk about old-school pizzerias like New Yorkers. The old places—Vesuvio, Via Mercanti, Danforth, Bitondo, and the like—were founded in the '50s and '60s. That makes them newcomers when seen through the lens of the American East Coast, São Paulo, or Buenos Aires.

There's not much in the way of pizza culture. Compared to Montreal, Toronto doesn't have a very old culinary history. It makes sense. As large cities go, it isn't old. Chatham, Ontario, an hour away, *is* somewhat infamous for the creation of Hawaiian pizza (at Satellite Restaurant), but that's another subject. Torontonians do tout their city as one of the world's most diverse. About half of its population is foreign-born, something you can't miss. Talk about diversity being a character of a culture—Toronto's is *all* about diversity. One cool thing about that is anything goes. People aren't as hung up about blending cultures and mashing up foods.

My first professional international pizza making was in Toronto in 2015 with Roberta's at a since-closed pizzeria called Citta. We tried to reproduce Roberta's pizza *exactly*. Learning how to do something the same way everywhere in different environments with different ingredients is a good skill. It was the first time we realized we would have to swap core ingredients—like using Canadian flour and cheese.

Canadian Flour Note

Canada Western Red Spring Wheat is a high-quality milled, hard wheat with high protein and great baking qualities. It's the most widely grown wheat in western Canada.

The second Toronto pop-up I did was on my own, a Thin & Crispy pop-up. I'd tested my take on bar pies at home, preparing for Uptown Social, a client in Charleston, South Carolina, requesting that style. Bar pizzas, if you haven't had them, are super thin, almost cracker-like (low-hydration dough) personal-sized pies mostly served at bars in the Northeast (the Midwest has thicker versions with more toppings).

I didn't care how anyone else did bar pizzas. I just knew I didn't want to do a low-hydration dough. What unifies my doughs is high hydration. You can make a crispy pizza with a high-hydration dough that has better flavor, so why not do that? Crackers are fine but not for pizza. I want structure and a pizza recognizable as bread, not just crunch. I want crunch and some chew.

So, I was working on my high-hydration dough and I upped the oil because oil softens bread. Think of brioche—soft and tender inside, crisp outside. I also felt if I upped the oil enough, the outside would fry slightly, harden, and crisp. It worked. This high-hydration, high-

oil mix became my Thin & Crispy dough. I was testing it and posting pictures of the cooked dough standing straight out with no tip sag on Instagram.

My friend and native Torontonian Dennis Chow saw the post and asked me to do a pop-up with his friends at Superpoint, Quebecois pizza slang for the tip of a slice. Denny is a graphic designer and home pizza maker with a pop-up company, Werewolf Pizza. I met him when he won the first Bushwick Block Party (we'd close the street and invite ten thousand of our closest friends) T-shirt design contest at Roberta's—arguably its best T-shirt design, and there were many.

You can look at a restaurant's Instagram and website, but you don't know what it or its people will be like until you visit. It could be a disaster. But I agreed to the pop-up.

It turns out Superpoint is a super cool restaurant that happens to sell New York–style pizza by the slice. The owners, Jesse Fader and Jonny Poon, are good guys and talented chefs who taught themselves how to make pizza when they opened in 2016. The food ranges from traditional Italian to Chinese to hearty Canadian. I learned a great trick while making dough there.

When I did that pop-up at Citta, we used Italian flour. But I didn't use 00 flour for Thin & Crispy. I wanted to use the American flour I'd been experimenting with. They didn't have it, so I had to find a similar Canadian flour. Jesse suggested visiting Blackbird Baking Co., an awesome shop that does great naturally leavened, hand-shaped bread. We asked baker Simon Blackwell, "What do you use for your basic all-purpose or bread flour?"

I figured if what they use works, it will work for pizza. He gave us a few bags of P&H Milling Group Canadian flour. It makes sense to use Canadian flour since Canada is one of the world's top ten largest wheat producers. But the dough acted differently. At first, I wasn't sure what happened, but the flour must have had a lower absorption rate, so it felt wet. But the pizzas Jesse and I made in that deck oven were amazing. Crisp, thin, and cracker-like with a little crumb.

I learned a few things. If the dough doesn't feel right, power through. We had to use extra flour to get it in the oven, but wet can be good. Sometimes you bake it and it comes out amazing. The dough at Sally's and Frank Pepe in New Haven looks like a puddle—it's a flat wet disc—but the pizza is beloved. It's better to be too wet than too dry, in my opinion. Sure, sometimes it can be hard to work with—difficult to shape—but the dough's flavor was amazing. This encouraged me to use local flour.

Thin & Crispy became a thing. People asked me to do Thin & Crispy pop-ups on New York's Lower East Side, in Los Angeles, Austin, Brooklyn, and all over. It was great because I'd never done that style on a large scale and I got to test it out for my client. A year later, when Uptown Social opened in 2018, I was confident in this pizza because I'd made it in a few different countries, with as many different flours, and better understood how it worked. It was important to fuck stuff up along the way to get to that outstanding final product.

GENERAL ASSEMBLY

Ali Khan Lalani is one of my earlier clients. I met Ali at the Superpoint pop-up and teamed with him to open General Assembly in Toronto in 2017. He was already working on General Assembly and wanted to involve me with recipe development, the menu, the layout.

We agreed on a contract, he sent me the layout, and I immediately told him to stop construction. The kitchen needed a redesign. To his credit, Ali had faith in my ability to design a pizza kitchen. He listened, and we reworked the design to include a custom pizza table with a double-sided topping station going into the oven. When it's busy, that thing cranks pizza out. It's nuts.

General Assembly's overall layout is great. There's a glass-encased room where you can see dough being made. It's a strikingly beautiful restaurant in Toronto's Entertainment District near the Rogers Centre where the Blue Jays play, and there are lots of bars, restaurants, and condos. Office workers come for lunch, folks come in before and after the ballgames, after drinking and shopping, and then you've got locals who make this their neighborhood dinner spot. On our busiest day we did over a thousand all naturally leavened pizzas.

lamb sausage pizza

Makes 1 (11-inch/28-cm) pizza

On paper, this seems crazy. I don't think I've ever been accused of being an orthodox pizza traditionalist, but I try to keep pizza connected to its tradition of Mediterranean roots and my Sicilian-American heritage. That said, flatbreads have been cooked for thousands of years, and all over the eastern Mediterranean, there's a dish called *lahm bi ajeen*, spiced meat on flatbread. When I was asked to do a lamb pizza in Toronto for General Assembly, I had this in mind.

One key to its success was a Lebanese woman on staff named Ayah. Her mom signed off on our sausage seasoning with minor changes. The final product was far from traditional lahm bi ajeen, but had all the things I want: history, modern updates, and a taste that's familiar and feels like it belongs but is different at the same time. It's bright, refreshing, satisfying, and crave-worthy. I'm proud of it.

30 grams (2 tablespoons) labneh or plain Greek yogurt
Juice of ½ lemon
1 (250-g) Neapolitanish dough ball (page 90)
56 grams (¼ cup) Basic Tomato Sauce (page 52)
Small (20 g) white onion, minced
40 g (about 1½ ounces) low-moisture mozzarella, shredded
Lamb Sausage (page 215)
Pinch za'atar
5 or 6 leaves flat-leaf parsley, finely chopped
8 leaves mint, finely chopped

1. Preheat your hacked oven (see page 265) to 550°F (288°C) or set your high-temperature oven to 850°F (454°C).

2. In a small bowl, combine the yogurt and lemon juice. Pour into a squeeze bottle and set aside.

3. Stretch out the dough according to the Neapolitanish method (see page 38).

4. Using a 2-ounce (60-ml) ladle or a large spoon, spread the tomato sauce evenly on the dough, leaving 1 inch (2½ cm) around the dough's circumference for the crust. Top with the onion and mozzarella. It should look light—it shouldn't be too cheesy.

5. Using your hands, pluck off small coin sized balls of sausage and distribute them on the pizza every 2 inches (5 cm), moving from the outside in. Dust with the za'atar.

6. Bake the pizza directly on the stones of your hacked home oven for about 5 minutes or until the crust is nicely browned, rotating halfway through. In your high-temp oven cook for about 2 minutes or until leopard-spotted, rotating halfway through.

7. Cut the pizza into 6 slices, and in a zigzag fashion, top with the yogurt mixture, then dust with the parsley and mint.

BRAZIL

I thank Brazil for making me an international pizza consultant.

I knew little about Brazil before visiting but can't imagine life without the friends and experiences I've made there.

My first visit was in 2015 to make pizza for Roberta's. We were hosted by the restaurant group Cia Tradicional do Comércio, kind of as ambassadors of Brooklyn. The first stop was Rio de Janeiro, the city and culture most Americans think of when they think of Brazil.

But Brazil is *huge* (just 13 percent smaller than America), and the next stop, São Paulo, was reminiscent of New York City (it even has its own Empire State Building). It's immediately apparent that there's a large Italian community and strong pizza culture.

Paulistanos call their city the "pizza capital of the world" (they can fight over that title with Old Forge, Pennsylvania). But considering only New York City has more pizzerias by total number, it's a valid claim.

I had no expectations. I heard stories about ketchup-topped pizza, like some bizarre alternative pizza universe. But when I hit the ground it all became clear.

Rio and São Paulo are completely different. Rio is older. São Paulo was nothing more than a village until the eighteenth century. Rio was the capital of the Portuguese empire from 1807 until 1822, with the royal court moving there briefly, and its food reflects this Portuguese influence. It's

delicious, and Rio is amazing, but judging Brazil's pizza game by Rio would be like judging America's by Miami.

São Paulo's first population expansion began with the discovery of gold in the nearby southeastern state of Minas Gerais in the seventeenth century. São Paulo became a jumping-off point for *bandeirantes,* fortune hunters seeking their fortune in the jungle. It was then that the first significant populations of enslaved people were brought from Africa to São Paulo. After that, mining and coffee plantations became the driving force of its economy. By the time slavery was abolished in 1888, the use of enslaved people's labor was already on the decline, and large populations of European, Arab, and Japanese immigrants were sought to do that plantation work.

The largest number of immigrants to São Paulo were Italians. Today there are more people of Italian ancestry in São Paulo than in Rome, Italy's most populous city.

Many of these Italians came from Campania and brought pizza with them, including to Castelões Cantina & Pizzaria, São Paulo's oldest.

There's *a lot* of pizza in São Paulo. They even do pizza *rodizio*, which, if you've ever been to a *churrascaria*, you'll infer as all-you-can-eat pizza where they come by with pies covered in crazy toppings until you can't think about another slice. In addition to all the pizza places I visited, I had a ton of pizzas delivered to my hotel late at night just to try them. They ranged from terrible to satisfyingly terrible. But Castelões was amazing.

With its red-checked tablecloths and Chianti bottles hanging from the ceiling, it's like discovering a long-lost, old-school pizzeria in the Bronx. It's a wood-fired pizza that's like a mix of Roman and Neapolitan styles. It comes out big and heavy with a puffy and slightly leopard-spotted crust. They're known for their pie with tomato sauce, mozzarella, thin-sliced Calabresa sausage, and oregano, a combination of toppings known at other São Paulo pizzerias as the Castelões.

Strangely, it's not on many pizza lists. It's changing, but there isn't the reverence for

Pizza Toppings in Brazil

Portuguese food tends to be rich and meat-heavy, and that influence translates to Brazilian pizzas, which are also heavy on olive oil. Their most popular pizzas are the Calabresa, a spicy sausage pie (their version of a pepperoni pizza); the Quatro Queijos, a white, four-cheese pie; and the Portuguesa (tomato, mozzarella, ham, onions, olives, and chopped hard-boiled eggs). This was a unique combination to me. Those pizzas are everywhere. You frequently see pizza with *catupiry*, a soft white, processed cheese that's like a smoother cream cheese version of Velveeta. It's not good, but it's been around since 1911. You'll also see pies with canned tuna and tomato sauce and endless dessert pizzas.

pizza history we have. I raved about Castelões and the response was, "The sad thing is it will probably close. People don't want old-school pizza, they want new-school places and pizza ordered through an app and delivered by bike." I think Castelões will have a renaissance, and that would be great because the history of places like this one is important.

Of the newer-school places, A Pizza da Mooca (in a very Italian neighborhood of that name that's said to have the highest number of pizzerias per inhabitant in São Paulo) was Neapolitanish and a favorite. Carlos Pizza in Vila Madalena, which counts among its partners Luciano Nardelli, who worked at D.O.M. (one of the world's best restaurants), makes a wood-fired Neapolitan-style pizza and also was very good.

We had incredible hosts, including Benny Novak, a great chef and one of Cia Tradicional do Comércio's partners, and especially Alexandra Forbes. If you need a fixer or food and travel expert in Brazil, Alexandra Forbes is it. She's a food and travel writer and columnist at *Folha de S.Paulo* (Brazil's biggest newspaper), and she showed us around to fine dining spots like D.O.M., which was incredible (so was hanging out, eating, and drinking with

D.O.M.'s chef, Alex Atala, in his apartment the next few days), and A Casa do Porco (the "House of the Pig"), named one of the world's best restaurants. But we also hit casual places and got to experience the beloved bar food at Bar Momo, Carioca soul food at Bar da Gema in Rio, and an incredible, late-night chicken and cachaça spot, Galeto Sat's.

Brazil is different from anywhere else. The people are terrific. Friendly, easygoing, funny, kind, generous, and great hosts, but direct when they want something. The chefs were the same and the food was amazing.

So many things were familiar but new. There are incredible chiles—something I grew up with in Tex-Mex and Mexican cuisines—and similarly, many black bean dishes. I'd never had *feijoada* (bean stew with beef and pork), and it blew my mind. And there are things you don't get unless you visit. The fruits, the meats (*picanha* on the grill!), their approach to both, manioc (a starchy root also known as cassava or yuca that's a staple of many dishes), *farofa* (toasted manioc flour that has the texture of breadcrumbs)...São Paulo is a massive, mind-blowing whirlwind.

At the birth of my pizza consultancy career, Benny and I reconnected about a project called Bráz Elettrica. The restaurant group already owned pizzerias and bars—they've been at it for some twenty years—but they needed something from me: a different kind of pizza, creative topping combinations, and the ability to build a

fast-casual program based on speed.

I went down with my sourdough starter, experimented with ingredients and the Izzo electric oven, worked through a menu, did a pizza party, and ninety days later . . . the first Bráz Elettrica opened in 2017 in Pinheiros ("the pine trees"), São Paulo's coolest neighborhood. Crucial to the success was our first hire, Paul Cho, a talented chef who still runs all seven locations of Bráz Elettrica. The New Portuguese Pizza (page 165) is the signature pizza that came out of this, but the Bolognese (page 162) and Brazilian Mashed Potato Pizza (page 182) are awesome too.

MAD BOLOGNA

This pizza is a great example of how to come up with well-balanced topping combinations. We created it in São Paulo at Bráz Elettrica. It may seem counterintuitive, but the strategy isn't to invent something, but to use classic flavor combinations and then apply a spin. I gravitate to traditional Italian flavors and combinations. There are all kinds of dishes with flavor combinations people love. If that translates to pizza, do it. The key is *translation*. You can't take ingredients in a dish and throw them on pizza. That's asshole shit I see all the time. Vegan mac and cheese pizza? No thanks. There are no rules, but there are things I'm not interested in. And if I *have* to do them, I'm doing them my way.

Traditional Bolognese lasagna is a fantastic dish when done correctly: Bolognese sauce, béchamel, Parmigiano, lasagna noodles, and sometimes mozzarella. Bolognese is an Italian meat sauce from Bologna, the capital of the Emilia-Romagna region, in Northern Italy, and one of the country's culinary centers. Béchamel is just a roux with flour, milk, butter, nutmeg, and salt. If you were to use that thick Bolognese sauce as the base, it would weigh it down. It would also be expensive because it requires more prep than your typical sauce. But it's delicious and a beautiful pizza—a great example of recreating components of a classic dish as pizza.

bolognese pizza

Makes 1 (11-inch/28-cm) pizza

We want the Bolognese, this thick meaty ragu, to brown a bit because that's one of the best parts of lasagna—the crusty top. We start with a basic tomato sauce, add buffalo mozzarella, use the Bolognese sporadically *on top*, then add a drizzle of béchamel. You want to make sure there are spots where you see *just* Bolognese and *just* béchamel—a textural and artful interplay between toppings—and lots of Parmigiano.

1 (250 g) Neapolitanish dough ball (page 90)

28 grams (2 tablespoons) Basic Tomato Sauce (page 52)

55 grams (about 2 ounces) fresh mozzarella

25 grams (about 1 ounce) Parmigiano-Reggiano, finely grated

15 grams (1 tablespoon) extra-virgin olive oil, in a squeeze bottle

25 grams (2 tablespoons) Bolognese Sauce (page 196)

25 grams (2 tablespoons) Béchamel Sauce (page 195), in a squeeze bottle

5 grams (about ¼ ounce) flat-leaf parsley, chopped

1. Preheat your hacked oven (see page 265) to 550°F (288°C) or set your high-temperature oven to 850°F (454°C).

2. Stretch out the dough according to the Neapolitanish method (see page 38).

3. Using a large spoon, spread the tomato sauce evenly on the dough, leaving 1 inch (2½ cm) around the dough's circumference for the crust.

4. Using your fingers, tear off quarter-sized chunks of mozzarella and top directly onto the pizza from the outside in, leaving about ¾ inch (2 cm) between each piece. Dust with half of the Parmigiano-Reggiano and, using a squeeze bottle, drizzle with the olive oil. Spoon the Bolognese sauce onto the pizza around the pieces of mozzarella.

5. Using a squeeze bottle, squeeze a zigzag of béchamel sauce across the whole pizza. Dust with the remaining Parmigiano-Reggiano.

6. Bake the pizza directly on the stones of your hacked home oven for about 5 minutes or until the crust is nicely browned, rotating halfway through. In your high-temp oven cook for about 2 minutes or until leopard-spotted, rotating halfway through.

7. Cut into 6 slices, top with the parsley, and serve.

the new portuguese pizza

Makes 1 (11-inch/28-cm) pizza

When I first got to Brazil, I was taken on a whirlwind food tour. After a few days, I wondered if anyone *ever* ate a salad. Considering how hot the weather was and how heavy the food is, everything I ate was amazing, but I noticed what made the Brazilian palate tick.

Adding eggs to proteins like steak or chicken is standard. So, when I got around to trying the most popular pizzas, I wasn't surprised by *pizza à Portuguesa*, aka *Portuguesa*, or, as we'd say, the Portuguese. Its toppings include tomato, mozzarella, oregano, loads of ham, copious sliced onion, olives, and sliced hard-boiled eggs—in character with bold flavors Brazilians love.

It was delicious, like a supreme Brazilian-style. When I started working on Bráz Elettrica's menu, I knew I wanted to do *my* take on the Portuguese. They dubbed it the Portuguese 2.0.

1 (250-g) Neapolitanish dough ball (page 90)

85 grams (about 3 ounces) fresh mozzarella

1 egg, yolk and white separated into individual squeeze bottles (page 189)

56 grams (¼ cup) Basic Tomato Sauce (page 52)

Pinch dried wild Sicilian oregano, stems removed

30 grams (about 1 ounce) Caramelized Onions (page 209)

30 grams (about 1 ounce) prosciutto cotto, thinly sliced and torn into small pieces

20 grams (about ¾ ounce) green olives, pitted and quartered

1. Preheat your hacked oven (see page 265) to 550°F (288°C) or set your high-temperature oven to 850°F (454°C).

2. Stretch out the dough according to the Neapolitanish method (see page 38).

3. Using your fingers, tear off coin sized chunks of mozzarella and top directly onto the pizza, leaving about ¾ inch (2 cm) between each piece. Squeeze the egg white among the mozzarella pieces.

4. Using a ladle or a large spoon, spread the tomato sauce using the *spulacci* technique (see page 37). Dust with the oregano. Working from the outside in, add the caramelized onions, then the prosciutto cotto, and then the green olives.

5. Bake the pizza directly on the stones of your hacked home oven for about 5 minutes or until the crust is nicely browned, rotating halfway through. In your high-temp oven cook for about 2 minutes or until leopard-spotted, rotating halfway through.

6. Cut the pizza into 6 slices, immediately drizzle the egg yolk onto the hot pizza in a zigzag fashion, and serve.

TOKYO

I started calling myself an international pizza consultant in 2017, after my first job consulting on pizza outside of America. But I didn't *feel* like one until I went to Tokyo.

I'd always wanted to go to Japan. I grew up in the '80s and '90s, and my whole life I've been into samurai, ninjas, and video games. I'd heard of Tokyo-style pizza but never had it. So I was excited when Abdullah Al Khabbaz, a new client, reached out about Tokyo-style pizza he wanted to do in Kuwait. Abdullah owns a restaurant management company called Nejoud with restaurants and coffee shops in Kuwait, Saudi Arabia, Bahrain, Qatar, and the Emirates. Working with professionals means I'll look good when the project succeeds after I'm gone.

I was on my way to the UK to do a pop-up at Yard Sale Pizza, a mini-chain in East London, doing a series of guest pizza makers. I told Abdullah I could meet him in New York, but he was London-bound and suggested we talk there. It was fun despite being detained at Gatwick Airport for eight hours on suspicion of visiting to work illegally. Eventually they determined what I was there to do was fine. I guess the immigration officer just didn't like "pizza party" as an answer when they asked why I was there.

Abdullah and I negotiated the contract, shook hands, and then he said we'd have to visit Japan to do research. Now I'm booking a flight to Tokyo.

A trip to London where I was doing a pop-up, where I'd also meet a client from Kuwait (who found me on Instagram) to talk about doing Tokyo-style pizza. If that doesn't make you feel like an international pizza consultant, what will?

Getting paid to travel to Japan to research pizza is a career highlight. But it's something I took seriously because I'd need to *recreate* this pizza in Kuwait, and if you know anything about how meticulous food is in Japan, you realize, as I knew, it would be tough.

The trip and the research helped me to understand *how* a style comes to be, what it is, and what it means to people.

I put on a T-shirt, met Abdullah in the lobby, and we started eating at fantastic pizza places beginning with Savoy, a tiny place nearby where you have to climb a staircase to the oven. The way the dough was pinched created little craters and char. The pizzas were uniquely shaped. There was a thin layer of crispiness on the outer crust, but inside it was fluffy. The dough was flavorful and aggressively seasoned. The salt crystals embedded underneath the pizza stood out. Like Neapolitan pies, this was a wet pizza, with lots of good olive oil, but that extra crispiness and saltiness made it unique. I don't say this lightly, but it was perfectly executed.

Next, we went to PST (Pizza Studio Tamaki) in Tokyo's Minato City (southwest of the Imperial Palace). There were similar idiosyncrasies, but PST does crazy toppings. About a fifteen-minute drive away in Meguro City is Pizzeria e Trattoria da ISA, a VPN-certified Neapolitan pizzeria. It could be in Italy. But you realize instantly, this is *excellent* Neapolitan pizza. Pizzaiolo Hisanori Yamamoto has done well at the World Pizza Cup competition in Naples.

But the true pilgrimage for Tokyo-style is Susumu Kakinuma's Seirinkan. When pizza guys talk, they eventually discuss Tokyo-style pizza—it's almost mythical—and inevitably, Kakinuma. The story is that as a young man backpacking around Italy, pizza blew him away. He tried to train there, but it didn't happen. Still, he understood the concepts, held on to his pizza memories, and returned to Japan.

The Japanese have a word, *ikigai*, which means "a reason for being," the idea of dedicating your life to perfecting one thing. They apply it to everything from sword making to sushi. Kakinuma decided pizza was his calling. He had an oven built based on what he saw in Naples but using Japanese stones. He opened Nakameguro Savoy in 1995 and established his reputation, then closed it and reopened in 2007 as Seirinkan ("House of Sacred Wood"), a shop unlike any other.

He only does a Margherita and a marinara, and he uses fantastic products (some Japanese, some Italian). His dough is soft, but crisp outside, and thicker. Instead of the Naples slap-and-fold technique, he pinches the dough, bunched up, imparting a starfish pattern. There are little points around the crust, unlike any other round pizza in the world. His toppings adhere to the Japanese aesthetic, which celebrates *fukinsei*, where the idea is balance via irregularity and asymmetry. With pizza this means mozzarella and basil perfectly placed and sauce equally applied is *not* as pleasing as Kakinuma's *seemingly* random but organized beauty, the asymmetry in nature that's pleasing to the eyes.

Kakinuma's Margherita features haphazard spoonfuls of crushed tomatoes; torn, coin sized mozzarella shreds; lots of olive oil; a giant basil pile in the middle, some under cheese, some under sauce; and that starfish-stretched dough. There are five distinct areas. There are little rivers of tomato with islands of mozzarella and areas *without*, where the crust has flattened and there was olive oil, creating this bubbly, charred bread. The sauce was smooth and saucy with charred tomato—it resembled uncrushed cherry tomatoes. Many places cube mozz, resulting in a melted cube look. This was amorphous and barely melted but browning from swimming in oil.

Another thing that defines Tokyo-style pizza? Salt. Kakinuma calls it a "salt punch," a sea salt sprinkling before the pizzas bake. They're cooked one at a time—it's not a high-volume operation—at high heat for a minute. There's beautiful blistering and the salt sticks to the *cornicione*, the edges, resulting in pretzel-like salty crust pieces. Kakinuma's pizzas are unique because they're made with presence. It's some of the best pizza ever. No pressure recreating that, right?

Then there's Kakinuma's marinara. The marinara is one of my favorite pizzas. It's about balance of sauce, oil, oregano, salt, and garlic. It's vegan but traditional. The bottom cooks nicely because extra sauce weighs it down. It also makes pizza a universal thing—that there are these two signatures of the original pizza.

Kakinuma has this round-tip serrated paring knife, and he slices a garlic clove super thin for each pizza *à la minute* (French for "as it happens")—I'm talking twenty-five slices of garlic(!). That's incredibly inefficient, but when garlic is the main part of the pizza, fresh is key. And that knife imparts ridges on the garlic slices, creating textural variance.

Kakinuma does things his way. He rests his peel on a high hat because he's a drummer, his oven is industrial steampunk, and one room is dedicated to the Beatles. He's not emulating Neapolitan pizzerias. Unlike da ISA, which transports you to Naples, Seirinkan transports you inside one man's brain.

People who Kakinuma trained have, in turn, opened pizzerias based on his techniques. So from the serrated paring knife to the crust pinching, this style is at Savoy and PST in Tokyo, Il Pappalardo in Kyoto, and others. Now it's known as Tokyo-style pizza, with Seirinkan as the foundation.

Sometimes that's how it starts—one person, crazy in the best possible way.

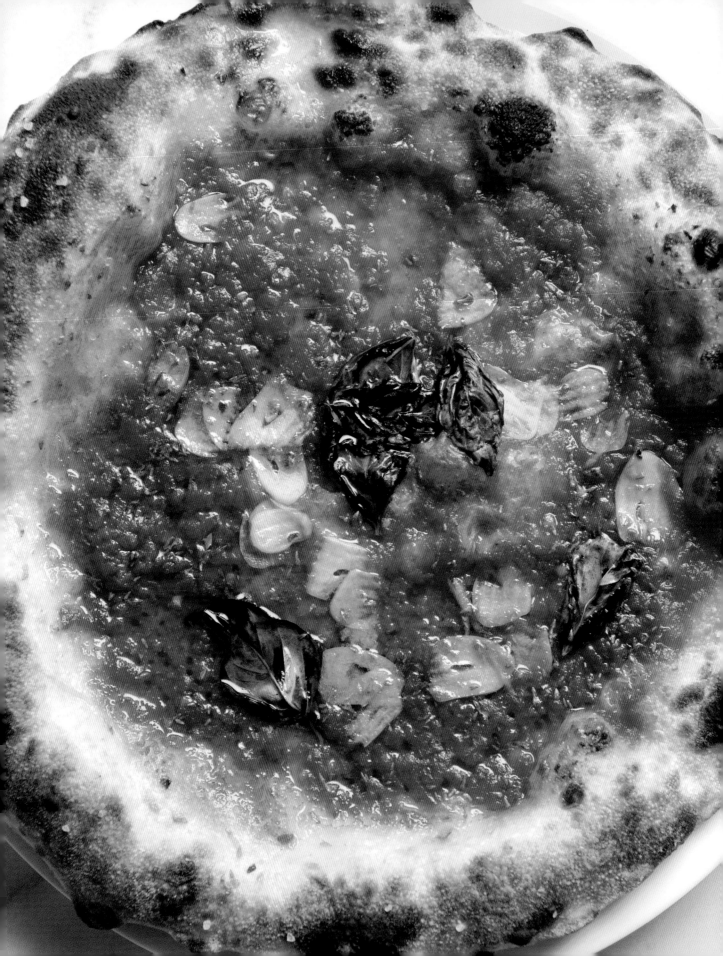

tokyo marinara

Makes 1 (11-inch/28-cm) pizza

---

1 (250-g) Neapolitanish dough ball (page **90**)

84 grams (6 tablespoons) Basic Tomato Sauce (page **52**)

1 clove garlic, peeled

Pinch dried wild Sicilian oregano, stems removed

6 basil leaves

15 grams (1 tablespoon) extra-virgin olive oil, plus more for topping, in a squeeze bottle

Pinch coarse sea salt

⚓ Falco Travel Tip

After a long international flight, I have a drill in my hotel room whenever I'm consulting. I unpack my medicine bag and put it in the bathroom, put my bag on the luggage carrier, set my laptop on the desk, then take a shower. I reset and try not to nap. If you arrive during the daytime, the idea is to stay up as long as you can and wear yourself out so you can sleep and get as in sync with the time difference as soon as possible. Sometimes a shower is as good as a nap.

1. Preheat your hacked oven (see page 265) to 550°F (288°C) or set your high-temperature oven to 850°F (454°C).

2. Stretch out the dough according to the Neapolitanish method (see page 38).

3. Using a ladle or a large spoon, spread the sauce evenly on the dough, leaving 1 inch (2½ cm) around the circumference for the crust. À la minute, use a serrated paring knife to thinly slice the garlic into the center of the pizza. Dust with the oregano.

4. Gently tear the basil leaves and place them evenly into the sauce. Using a squeeze bottle and starting from the outside in, drizzle with the olive oil. Crushing the salt between your fingers, dust the entire pizza, including the crust.

5. Bake the pizza directly on the stones of your hacked home oven for about 5 minutes or until the crust is nicely browned, rotating halfway through. In your high-temp oven cook for about 2 minutes or until leopard-spotted, rotating halfway through.

6. Cut the pizza into 6 pieces and top with an additional drizzle of olive oil.

THAILAND

Bangkok is the world's most visited city. It's cosmopolitan with lots of expats. Clearly, Thai food is popular (and you can find regional food from all over Thailand in Bangkok), but there's also great Chinese, Japanese, Italian, and Indian food—it's a culinary capital. I first visited as a backpacker in my early twenties and then in 2010 with my wife on our honeymoon, and it's one of my favorite cities. So, it was exciting to work there.

There are a lot of Italians in Thailand and so lots of Italian-style pizza, everything from Roman thin crust to Neapolitan. There are people making mozzarella and Italians (and Thais for that matter) with mozzarella companies. There's even Tokyo-style Neapolitan.

Chain pizza is well represented. One of Thailand's biggest chain pizzas is The Pizza Company. It started as a Pizza Hut franchise, but when their agreement ended, they changed the name. I was blown away because they do the "Pizza Hut" pan pizza and it's the way Pizza Hut *used* to be. It's like going back in time to when Pizza Hut was good. They're all over Thailand, but also in Cambodia, China, Saudi Arabia, Jordan, Laos, Vietnam—there are over five hundred locations globally. Thailand's a player in the pizza world.

All of that makes it a good place to make pizza because you're not starting from scratch. There is an infrastructure for pizza ingredients and equipment. I went as a consultant for my client Rohit Sachdev to help with an underrepresented style in Thailand, the New York City slice. There haven't been that many great New York City–style slice joints outside America in my experience, but it's having a global moment.

Rohit is from Thailand, where he's managing director for Soho Hospitality, which operates several restaurants in Bangkok. But Rohit went to NYU and lived in New York City for many years. When he returned, he missed access to a great slice.

Soho Pizza opened in 2019 and does brisk business serving late-night slices for partygoers. We developed 18-inch (45-cm) pizzas cooked in a PizzaMaster Electric Oven. An interesting thing about this project was that most of the ingredients I found there were either for doing chain pizzas or Neapolitan pies. There wasn't a lot of high-protein bread flour, usually where you want to start with New York–style pizza. I blended Italian and French flours to mimic American bread flour. We did a custom cheese blend to mimic Grande pizza cheese and a hybrid of commercial yeast and sourdough starter.

It's a fantastic New York slice. Straightforward but with inventive flavors. Expats love it. A retired cop from Jersey who visited said it was some of the best pizza he'd ever had. Mission accomplished.

It's a Small (Pizza) World After All

We had just started taste-testing pizzas for Soho Pizza when I saw on Instagram that my friend and possibly the most knowledgeable pizza expert in New York City, Scott Wiener, was *also* in Bangkok! He was a welcome addition to our tasting, and after a long day of eating pizza, which we both do for a living, we went to Havana Social, Rohit's award-winning rum bar down the street. Nice work if you can find it.

AMYLASE
AND
PROTEASE

You already know I was one of the kids joking about Butt Krust (see page 136), so I won't pretend I'm a scientist. But if you like to geek out over making pizza, it's helpful to know a few basic things about these two enzymes.

Amylase occurs naturally in flour because wheat kernels need to break down their own starch into sugar for energy when they germinate. Amylase comes in two kinds, alpha- (which randomly breaks the sugar-starch chain into smaller pieces), and beta- (which breaks bits off the end of the chain). It's the first enzyme to act in dough and it's activated by water. As I've since come to understand it (thanks, Scientific American!), this is why higher hydration doughs ferment faster: The moisture enables the enzymes to get around better.

Then there's the protease enzyme, which is a little like dark matter—people have been debating its existence and importance for years. Supposedly, it helps break up gluten, softening your dough. Both enzymes are also said to have an effect on the flavor of your dough and can contribute to the browning that happens during baking.

PORTLAND

I stirred up controversy in the pizza world in 2018 while cooking pizza at Feast Portland, an amazing annual Pacific Northwest food festival in Portland, Oregon. Food is great all along the West Coast but especially delicious in the Pacific Northwest. Portland is special among West Coast cities because it has one of the best pizza cultures in America.

Portland is the intersection of pizza greatness: wheat grown and milled in the Pacific Northwest and terrific produce grown year-round in a Mediterranean climate. Cooking in Portland is like what I'd imagine it's like to cook in the Mediterranean, with farmers and millers who care about food and food systems. Because of

this, the food is great. I get excited about cooking with great product. I tried to explain this to a journalist and it got me into trouble.

I was making pizza under a tent on a rainy day with Tusk chef Sam Smith for Feast's annual kickoff party. People were talking to me while I worked. I was worried about my dough, which was under-proofed. Normally I mix, rest, mix, then bulk at room temperature. Because of space constraints, I couldn't leave the dough out overnight. So I put it in the fridge. The fermentation never got rolling, a problem when there's no commercial yeast in your dough (not much will happen in the fridge and it will be slow to restart). Usually you can warm it up, but

it was Portland in September, so it was cold and wet—the dough time and human time weren't working out.

I was using an organic hard wheat flour called Edison that was new to me. It's milled in the Willamette Valley by Camas Country Mill, and everyone told me to be careful of its "enzymatic activity."

Frankly, I didn't know what that meant. I know a lot of talented bakers and pizza people, and they come at me with this technical stuff. Some of it I know. Some of it I don't. I'm never afraid to say I have no idea what they're talking about. They told me the flour was freshly milled, that a lot of the grain was included in the flour, and that along with the naturally occurring wild yeast you'd expect on any flour, Edison was also high in *amylase* and *protease*.

The amount of amylase can vary depending on weather and other farming conditions, so my takeaway was that this flour was high in naturally occurring yeast and enzymes that feed fermentation. I'd always rather have over-proofed dough than under-proofed dough, just like I'd rather have wetter dough than dryer dough. Over-proofed, wetter doughs have more flavor. They're just tougher to work with.

Whatever. The pizzas were great.

I was happy with the local Camas Country Mill Edison flour (it tasted good and sat well in the stomach). I had beautiful, local,

in-season roasted chanterelles. Great cheese. Everything was gorgeous.

The event was packed, we were making pizzas like crazy, and this person starts asking me what I think about Portland's pizza scene. He did *not* identify himself as a reporter and asked me how Portland compared to New York City. I'd traveled to Portland twice over two weeks, visited three of its top pie spots (Apizza Scholls, Lovely's Fifty Fifty, and Scottie's Pizza Parlor), and had been impressed so I said as much. He kept pushing, so I said, "I think right now Portland is the greatest pizza city in America."

He was like, "What! Better than New York?"

Not surprisingly, in the age of listicles and viral sound-bites, the nuance of what I was trying to say was subsumed by the superlative. I was trying to convey a combination of things:

1. Ingredients: The Mediterranean climate and the ingredients it avails—quality wheat that's freshly milled and wonderful year-round produce—provide resources to Portland that give it an inherent advantage for making great pizza.

2. A Better Way: Portland has a history (though recent) of great pizzerias doing things the right way as a foundation—starting with Apizza Scholls.

Brian Spangler started Apizza Scholls in 2005. He's a wicked smart baker who can speak technically about his craft but decided to get out of bread baking and open a pizzeria. He does what he calls an East Coast pizzeria–style pizza. His cheese pizza is technically perfect. There's a big, thin, crispy crust separate from the sauce and the cheese. And he does mozzarella first, sauce on top, like old-school New York places. Brian uses great flour and everything from the crumb, crust, toppings, sauce, cheese, sauce-to-cheese ratio, sauce application, and the specials he runs that feature local produce are terrific. The big wooden booths you associate with pizza memories from being a kid, the classic '80s arcade games, the design—it's a perfect pizzeria.

Anthony Bourdain visited Apizza Scholls in 2006 for his Travel Channel show *No Reservations*, and called it some of America's best pizza. I think it's one of America's top five pizzas. I judge pizza on its dough. *That's* the hard part. For a cheese pizza, everything else should be straightforward: good tomatoes, quality mozzarella, but most important is the dough in the right proportions. The *dough* is the art. The science.

If you've opened a pizzeria in Portland since 2005, Apizza Scholls has to be in the

back of your mind—the eight hundred–pound pizza in the dough room. Why would you open a pizzeria nearby if you're not going to bring it? Brian has contributed to an overall higher level of quality. If you're opening in Portland, you gotta bring your A-game. People have.

After a restaurant like Apizza Scholls opens, the people it employs change the culinary landscape over time. This is how the restaurant business, and, definitely, the pizza world, work: People work at established, respected, and, if they're lucky, groundbreaking places, then start their own. Great restaurants create a genetic code, a culinary DNA, that goes on to make up a town.

New York City's known as a great pizza town, right? Well, there's nothing about New York City, out of everywhere in America, that made it a great place for Italian immigrants to make that happen. The climate is nothing like Southern Italy's. It just happened that's where they went. If there's great pizza, it's because of culture. Somebody started a great pizzeria, then someone who worked there left and opened a place. The *original* international pizza consultant, Filippo

Milone, opened a bunch of pizza places starting in the 1890s including what would come to be known as the original Lombardi's. Then a guy leaves Lombardi's and opens Totonno's in 1924. Allegedly, another guy leaves in 1933 and opens Patsy's. You have this history of people who want to make their own pizza. Maybe they even aspire to make it better than the place they worked, or better than the place everyone looks to as a pizza paragon.

Apizza Scholls is that foundation for Portland's pizza scene.

Now other places strive to raise the bar. Chef Sarah Minnick has since opened Lovely's Fifty Fifty (in 2009), where she takes seasonality and locality to the next level, making beautiful-looking, colorful, and delicious vegetable-forward pizzas with great dough using awesome flour combinations. They're different from Apizza Scholls (and Sarah's self-trained) but outstanding.

Then there's Scottie's Pizza Parlor (established in 2015), which does naturally leavened slices using great ingredients. It stacks up to anything in New York City. Scottie Rivera uses the high-temperature PizzaMaster ovens I love (that's where I first saw them).

Because they're not bound by the tradition that New York City or New Haven have, Portland pizza makers can take big chances. Then other places in Portland have to contend with *those* places . . . it creates a pizza scene. Remember Susumu Kakinuma and Seirinkan? The pizzeria he opened in Tokyo that created that pizza scene? Apizza Scholls is like that. In a way, everyone who comes after these pioneers is making a commentary on the original place.

I don't know that I would say there's a specific *style* of pizza in Portland. If there *is*, it's that everyone uses high-quality ingredients and makes vegetable-forward pizzas. Otherwise, when it comes to crusts or ovens, everyone does different stuff.

But back to the conversation at Feast. The guy wrote a click-baity article that lost the point of what I was saying. Which is a shame, because what I was trying to do was highlight great people doing cool things with fantastic ingredients. I wanted to bring attention to a highly functioning regional food system that connects local producers and farmers to independent pizzerias. All press is good press, I guess.

Bulking Dough

Bulking dough just means you have a large batch you're allowing to proof together, that you haven't cut up into dough balls yet. I do short (less than an hour) or up to twenty-four-hour long bulk fermentations.

"CONTROVERSIAL" PIZZAS

PINEAPPLE ON PIZZA

Pineapple pizza wasn't something I was ever into or passionately against. Just something *other* people did. Fast-forward to Toronto in 2018 when my client Ali Khan Lalani asked me to come up with one.

If you don't know, "Hawaiian" pizza was first popularized in 1962 by Sam Panopoulos, a Greek immigrant who owned restaurants in Ontario. He's the "evil mastermind" who hooked Canadians on the ham and pineapple combination. When you look at pizza menus in Canada, Hawaiian is up there with pepperoni and supreme as most popular.

Let me say before going further that I understand some native Hawaiians take offense at the usage and association of the word "Hawaiian" with this pizza. I acknowledge that and use the name for referential purposes only.

I liked the idea of reimagining pineapple pizza. I had an idea for a pizza version of *tacos al pastor*, itself a reimagined form of shawarma brought by Lebanese immigrants to Mexico. I took pineapple inspiration from a dish at Cosme in New York City where they make a tacos al pastor with fish instead of pork and use pineapple puree instead of chunks off the spit.

I threw whole pineapples in the pizza oven until the outsides were black, the insides were cooked, and their flavor was concentrated. After they cooled, we carved off the char and pureed the roasted fruit. I followed the al pastor road for a classic Old World and New World mashup.

I wasn't thinking about haters when I made this, but maybe I subconsciously made it extra delicious as a shield to criticism? Luckily, I was in Canada. It became a top seller. My takeaway? Don't take ingredients for granted. This pizza was such a great combination of sweet, savory, spicy, and velvety-crunchy, it made me a pineapple believer. By reducing and concentrating the flavor and combining it with complementing flavors and textures, it becomes a delicious, balanced pie.

Haters can order something else. It's their loss.

pineapple pizza al pastor—style

Makes 1 (13-inch/33-cm) pizza

The key to this pizza is the base layer of beautiful pineapple puree. I like doing puree on the bottom, then cheese, yellow onions, and, last, pork. The pineapple and cheese should blend to make this a golden, cheesy, melted situation. If you do decide to do chunks of pineapple, they should be between pieces of pork surrounded by flavor enhancers. No matter what, the lime-pickled onions get added post-bake.

**1 (250-g) Thin & Crispy dough ball
(page 63)**
**30 grams (3 tablespoons)
Pineapple Sauce (page 200)**
**55 grams (about 2 ounces)
low-moisture mozzarella, shredded**
**14 grams (1 tablespoon)
Basic Tomato Sauce (see page 52)**
**15 grams (about ½ ounce)
yellow onion, diced**
**40 grams (about 1½ ounces)
Al Pastor Pork (page 208)**
**20 grams (about ¾ ounce)
pickled jalapeño**
**2 grams (about ¹⁄₁₀ ounce) cilantro,
finely chopped**
**20 grams (about ¾ ounce)
Lime Pickled Onions (page 210)**

1. Preheat the oven with pizza stones to your oven's highest temperature setting (usually 550°F/288°C).

2. Stretch out the dough according to the Thin & Crispy method (see page 38).

3. Using a squeeze bottle or spoon, spread the pineapple sauce on the pizza, leaving 1½ inch (38 mm) around the dough's circumference for the crust.

4. Spread the mozzarella over the whole pizza.

5. Sprinkle the yellow onion evenly over the pizza.

6. Using a large spoon, spread the tomato sauce using the *spulacci* technique (see page 37).

7. Starting from the outside in, finish with the pork and jalapeños.

8. Bake the pizza directly on the pizza stone for 5½ minutes, or until the crust is nicely browned, checking the bottom and rotating it halfway through for an evenly colored crust.

9. Cut the pizza into 6 slices and top with the cilantro and lime-pickled onions.

POTATOES AND PIZZA
MASHED POTATO PIZZA

Putting mashed potatoes on pizza is a slightly assholeish thing to do—you're topping carbs with . . . more carbs—but when it works, it's comforting and slightly naughty stoner food turned up to eleven. It's also something chain pizzerias would do. Like mashed potato–loaded potato skin pizza (the first mashed potato pizza I made was a loaded potato skin pizza with speck, a beautiful Vermont Cheddar, and freshly chopped chives, and it was amazing).

If you *do* put mashed potatoes on a pizza, they should be fucking awesome.

I love mashed potatoes. It was the first dish I learned to cook. My mom is incredible and tough—I got my work ethic and tenacity from her—unfortunately, she bought into the propaganda that margarine is better than butter (it's not) and she wasn't good at making mashed potatoes. She had moments—there *were* times they were pretty good—but mostly . . . not so much. (Sorry, Mom.)

I wanted to know *why* Mom's mashed potatoes were great occasionally (light, fluffy, creamy, and buttery) and terrible (gummy, glutinous, heavy, and wet) the rest of the time. I asked people, I fixated on Alton Brown's *Good Eats* mashed potatoes episode "This Spud's for You," and I skimmed cookbooks.

Tricks for Totally Awesome

MASHED POTATOES

Here are tricks gleaned over the years that increase the consistency of achieving awesome mashed potatoes:

Yukon Gold

These dense yellow potatoes aren't starchy and work great.

Peeled

I like skins but not too many, especially because we'll use a bag to pipe onto the pizza and skins catch in the nozzle.

Cut Them Uniformly

It ensures even cooking.

Don't Overcook

Boil just until they're fork-tender.

Drain and Dry

Drain and spread the potatoes in a thin layer on a half sheet pan to dry them. It helps with fluffiness.

Rice Your Potatoes

Never use a food processor or blender. A blade will make potatoes gummy. You can use a food mill, but buy a ricer if you don't have one. You'll never look at homemade mashed potatoes the same.

Seasoning

I like seasoning potatoes with salt while they cook. Pepper and nutmeg are great and a little garlic isn't the worst thing that's ever happened.

Butter and Cream

Always use real butter and cream instead of milk and heat the two together with salt before adding them to the potatoes.

Gently combine the melted butter and cream mixture with riced potatoes and boom, best mashed potatoes ever.

brazilian mashed potato pizza

Makes 1 (9-inch/23-cm) pizza

---

1 (250-g) Neapolitanish dough ball (page 90)
55 grams (about 2 ounces) fresh mozzarella
60 grams (about 2 ounces) Mashed Potatoes (page 218), in a piping bag
1 egg, white and yolk separated, in individual squeeze bottles (see page 189)
25 grams (about 1 ounce) pancetta, thinly sliced
Pinch of chopped chives
2 pinches freshly ground black pepper

After you get over any hang-up about putting them on pizza, you realize the many possibilities potatoes present. I came up with this mashed potato and egg pizza at Bráz Elettrica in Brazil called the Supertramp Pizza. Mashed potatoes and eggs pair well. Add crispy pancetta and you have something special.

1. Preheat your hacked oven (see page 265) to 550°F (288°C) or set your high-temperature oven to 850°F (454°C).

2. Stretch out the dough according to the Neapolitanish method (see page 38).

3. Using your fingers, tear off coin sized chunks of mozzarella, and starting from the outside in, top directly onto the pizza, leaving about ¾ inch (2 cm) between each piece.

4. Using the piping bag, pipe small coin sized dollops of mashed potatoes in the gaps among the cheese.

5. Using a squeeze bottle and starting from the outside in, fill in the remaining spaces with the egg white, then cover the dough and toppings with the pancetta.

6. Bake the pizza directly on the stones of your hacked home oven for about 5 minutes or until the crust is nicely browned, rotating halfway through. In your high-temp oven cook for about 2 minutes or until leopard-spotted, rotating halfway through.

7. Cut the pizza into 6 slices, then using a squeeze bottle, drizzle with the egg yolk in a zigzag fashion. Top with the chives and black pepper.

EGGPLANT PIZZAS

Eggplant is an example of a seasonal ingredient that you don't want to try to reinvent the wheel with. Italians have had their hands on eggplant for a while and have done fantastic work with it. As a Sicilian-American, eggplant is a thing. You probably recognize a few renowned dishes: caponata, eggplant Parmigiana, and pasta alla Norma—great dishes.

The first eggplant pizza I put on a menu was a simple translation from a pasta I had in Sicily. Taking a tried-and-true pasta and translating it to pizza is a great trick. Pasta alla Norma is a dish that seems simple but is also mind-blowing. I came to understand it with this eggplant pizza.

So, ricotta salata . . . you can't put it into the oven. It doesn't melt. Ricotta salata *can* be used to finish, but not as the main cheese. It needs help. Enter mozzarella. A lot of pizzerias don't have fryers, so instead of fried chunks, I roast the hell out of the eggplant. Pair that with basic sauce, mozzarella, and Parmigiano, then out of the oven hit it with ricotta salata, breadcrumbs, and parsley to make it look nice and add texture—outstanding. It's not pasta alla Norma on pizza. It's the concept of pasta alla Norma *translated* to pizza.

Eggplant Seasonality

A note on eggplant seasonality: The first time I made this, I was getting great eggplants in August from New Jersey. Everyone loved the pizza, then the eggplants started disappearing in the market. When they vanished I eighty-sixed the pizza.

A regular asked, "Why'd you take that eggplant pizza off the menu? It was the best I've ever had!" Welp, that's it, isn't it? That was seasonal eggplant. They love hot, humid weather, and in the Northeast, that's a short season. Sure, you can get eggplant at the supermarket year-round. Maybe it's from a hothouse or shipped from some perpetually warm climate. Either way, the flavor of in-season eggplant versus out-of-season is night and day.

Look, it's difficult to be seasonal year-round, otherwise you'll be serving root vegetables and digging around the pantry for pickled and canned things all winter. It's no fun to be the hyper-seasonal, hyper-local garden cop, but like its solanum (nightshade) cousin the tomato, the difference is so huge that as a rule, I try only to cook with in-season eggplant.

eggplant parm pizza

Makes 1 (11-inch/28-cm) pizza

The secret to the best eggplant Parm pizza is making it in season. If it's January and you're making this pizza, you'd better be in South America. Okay, so it's eggplant season—in the Northeastern US, where I live, eggplant season tends to be July to October. Now how to make the best eggplant pizza? By using fresh, local, and delicious eggplant and seasoning it and every component that interacts with it—the sauce and the breadcrumbs. You'll use the breadcrumb recipe from this book. When you start with mind-blowing breadcrumbs and mind-blowing eggplant, you're set up for success.

56 grams (¼ cup) Basic Tomato Sauce (page 52)

1 (250-g) Neapolitanish dough ball (page 90)

3 Fried Eggplant Cutlets (page 214), cut into strips

4 to 5 leaves basil, torn

30 grams (about 1 ounce) provolone, shredded

55 grams (about 2 ounces) fresh mozzarella

25 grams (about 1 ounce) Pecorino-Romano, finely grated

20 grams (1½ tablespoons) extra-virgin olive oil, in a squeeze bottle

1. Preheat your hacked oven (see page 265) to 550°F (288°C) or set your high-temperature oven to 850°F (454°C).

2. Stretch out the dough according to the Neapolitanish method (see page 38).

3. Using a 2-ounce (60-ml) ladle or a large spoon, spread the tomato sauce evenly on the dough, leaving 1 inch (2½ cm) around the dough's circumference for the crust.

4. Top with the fried eggplant strips, basil, and provolone.

5. Using your fingers, tear off quarter-sized chunks of mozzarella and, starting from the outside in, top directly onto the pizza, leaving about ¾ inch (2 cm) between each piece.

6. Bake the pizza directly on the stones of your hacked home oven for about 5 minutes or until the crust is nicely browned, rotating halfway through. In your high-temp oven cook for about 2 minutes or until leopard-spotted, rotating halfway through.

7. Cut the pizza into 6 slices, top with the Pecorino, and, using a squeeze bottle, drizzle (from the outside in) with the olive oil.

pizza alla norma

Makes 1 (13-inch/33-cm) pizza

---

1 (250-g) Thin & Crispy dough ball (page 63)
60 grams (about 2 ounces) Roasted Eggplant (page 223)
55 grams (about 2 ounces) fresh mozzarella
4 leaves basil, torn
56 grams (¼ cup) Spicy Grandma Sauce (see page 56)
12½ grams (about ½ ounce) Sourdough Breadcrumbs (page 226)
25 grams (about 1 ounce) Parmigiano-Reggiano, finely grated
10 grams (¾ tablespoon) extra-virgin olive oil, in a squeeze bottle
20 grams (about ¾ ounce) ricotta salata, finely grated
Pinch parsley, finely chopped
Lemon zest

The key to pizza alla Norma is not too much eggplant. You don't want it to be dry, but you don't want to overload it. I've seen this pizza made where it's like, *Boom!*, heavy dose of eggplant! It ends up a soggy mess. It should be just enough so it's not dry and you get a little eggplant in every bite.

1. Preheat the oven with pizza stones to your oven's highest temperature setting (usually 550°F/288°C).

2. Stretch out the dough according to the Thin & Crispy method (see page 38).

3. Dollop silver dollar–sized chunks of roasted eggplant evenly over the dough and flatten them with the back of a spoon.

4. Using your fingers, tear off quarter-sized chunks of mozzarella and, from the outside in, top directly onto the pizza, leaving about ¾ inch (2 cm) between each piece. Top with the torn basil.

5. With a 2-ounce (60-ml) ladle or a large spoon, spread the arrabbiata sauce using the *spulacci* technique (see page 37). From the outside in, dust with the breadcrumbs and Parmigiano-Reggiano, and using a squeeze bottle (again, from the outside in), drizzle with the olive oil.

6. Bake the pizza directly on the pizza stone for 5½ minutes, or until the crust is nicely browned, checking the bottom and rotating it halfway through for an evenly colored crust.

7. Cut the pizza into 6 slices and top with the ricotta salata. Finish with the parsley and some lemon zest.

EGGS ON PIZZA:
THE SELMAN TECHNIQUE

When I first started making pizza professionally, I was working with a wood-fired oven. We did eggs on pizza from the beginning. Since then, I've topped thousands of pizzas with eggs. But nothing has changed: from that first egg to now, dread and anxiety have, and still do, come over me every time a ticket requests adding an egg. So much can go wrong. Let's walk through the missteps.

You crack the egg directly on the pizza, a *terrible* idea. You could miss some shell and ruin someone's meal. The other possibility? The yolk breaks. Now you're scooping up egg, then starting over. Don't be a hero. Crack the egg in a cup instead. Genius, right? Now your egg will be perfect before it's placed. But now you need to place it without breaking it, then get the pizza to the oven—two *more* opportunities for disaster. The egg needs a nest in the center safe from sharp toppings like onion slices. Remember, that egg will slide en route to the oven. If it hits those spears, game over.

Okay, you made it *to* the oven. But the pie needs to be launched. If you shove the pizza in full speed, the momentum will slide that egg off and onto the oven floor. I've done it more than I care to remember. Let's say you perfectly crack the egg, safely nestle it, get the pizza to the oven, launch it, and it's pretty much centered, yolk intact. *Now* all you have to do is cook the pizza perfectly *and* time that to the egg whites being cooked with a runny yolk.

Even if you avoid these pitfalls, now what? Do you cut and serve the pizza with a pool of runny yolk in the middle that unevenly distributes itself in the direction(s) of *its* choice, a tiny piece of egg on the tip of each slice? Or do you serve the pizza uncut? Uncut is always a copout. Maybe you could break the yolk *after* it comes out of the oven and move it all around so a little egg covers the entire pie. That sounds nice.

What if I told you there's a way to achieve egg on every slice, perfectly cooked whites, and runny yolk? Let me explain the Selman technique.

David Selman was a chef I worked with at Roberta's. We were experimenting with brunch pizzas and trying to solve having to refire egg pizzas when he came up with this. Now, Chef Selman is a smart guy. I doubt he was first to figure this out, but he showed me so we're calling this the Selman technique. I have taken it around the world, and people love it because it's basic but brilliant.

You separate eggs and fill a squeeze bottle full of whites, and another with yolks. Your pizza gets topped and then you squeeze whites over everything before it goes in. When the hot pizza comes out with fully cooked fluffy whites, you slice it. *Then* you squirt raw yolks in a lattice or squiggle pattern.

You get both parts of egg on every bite. Beautiful.

eggs for pizza

Makes 1 egg for use on 1 pizza

1 egg
2 small pinches sea salt, 1 for whites and 1 for yolks

I don't do swirls—I think it looks silly—so I advise lattice. If you're worried about salmonella, I've temped yolks at just under 140°F (60°C) on the surface of a hot pizza. They are runny but they *are* cooked. You can easily scale this recipe up by adding another egg for each additional pizza you're making.

1. Separate the whites and yolks into 2 small bowls.

2. Whisk the salt into the white and transfer it to a squeeze bottle.

3. Repeat with the yolk in a separate bottle. Keep the bottles in the fridge until it's time to cook pizza.

potato, egg, and cheese pizza

Makes 1 (11-inch/28-cm) pizza

I used to teach a Sunday morning pizza class with Pete Litschi, my best friend and business partner, at The Brooklyn Kitchen in Williamsburg. Every class we'd go over O.G. pizzas and come up with a new one. It was a way to try ideas, pressure free. If the students loved one, we knew we were onto something. One of the things students always ask about is eggs on pizza, so we experimented a lot with eggs. This potato, egg, and Cheddar pizza was one of the winners.

1 (250-g) Neapolitanish dough ball (page 90)

55 grams (about 2 ounces) fresh mozzarella

4 Fingerling Potatoes (page 210), torn into bite-size pieces

20 grams (about ¾ ounce) Cheddar, shredded

Eggs for Pizza (page 189), in 2 squeeze bottles

25 grams (about 1 ounce) Tomatillo Sauce (page 199), in a squeeze bottle

Pinch sea salt

25 grams (about 1 ounce) Speck 'n' Bits (see below)

5 grams (about ¼ ounce) scallions, thinly sliced

Pinch cilantro, finely chopped

1. Preheat your hacked oven (see page 265) to 550°F (288°C) or set your high-temperature oven to 850°F (454°C).

2. Stretch out the dough according to the Neapolitanish method (see page 38).

3. Using your fingers, tear off coin sized chunks of mozzarella, and starting from the outside in, top directly onto the pizza, leaving about ¾ inch (2 cm) between each piece. Filling in the spots among the pieces of cheese, repeat with the fingerling potatoes and then the Cheddar.

4. Using a squeeze bottle and starting from the outside in, fill in the spaces with the egg white. Repeat with the tomatillo salsa, then season with the salt.

5. Bake the pizza directly on the stones of your hacked home oven for about 5 minutes or until the crust is nicely browned, rotating halfway through. In your high-temp oven cook for about 2 minutes or until leopard-spotted, rotating halfway through.

6. Cut the pizza into 6 slices. Using a squeeze bottle, drizzle with egg yolk in a zigzag fashion, then top with the sliced scallions, speck 'n' bits, and cilantro.

Speck 'n' Bits

On a baking sheet or raised rack, bake slices of speck in a 450°F (232°C) oven for approximately 5 minutes or until crispy. Once cool, crumble by hand.

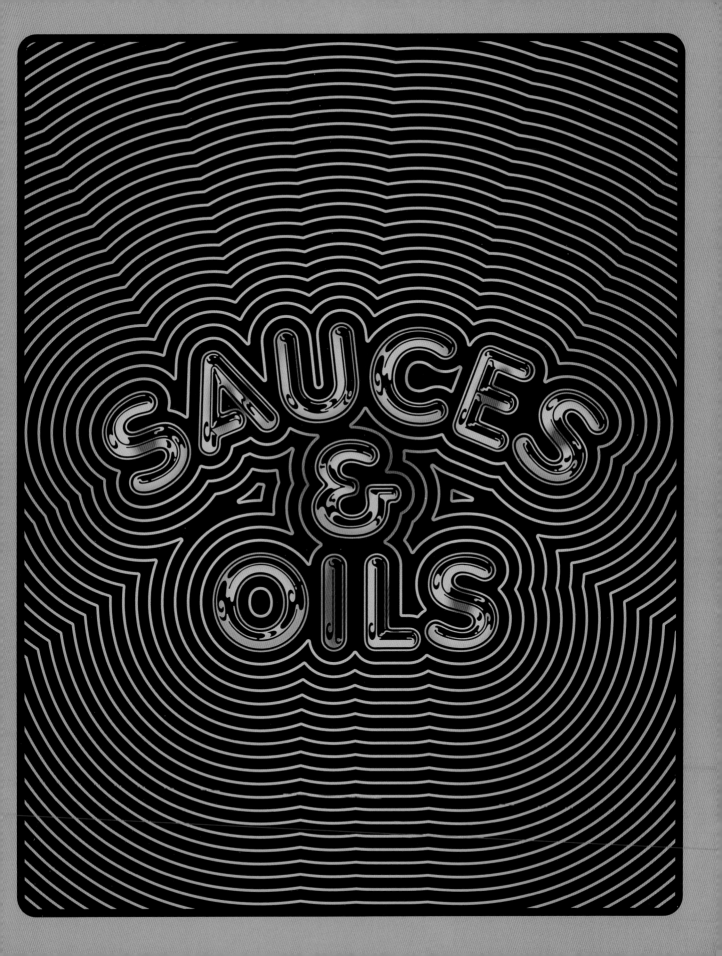

anchovy sauce

Makes 1 quart (about 1 liter)

This is the anchovy pizza sauce for people who don't think they like anchovies. It's a great way to use them, as a subtle component of a sauce instead of full-on fillets where you get those big flavor explosions. The key is to break down the anchovies. They'll bubble and dissolve into the oil, concentrating their savory, umami flavor. This will be delicious on Sicilian grandma dough, but you could put it on any of the pizza styles featured in this book, and it would be great with pasta.

**1 (794-gram/28-ounce)
can whole tomatoes, drained
110 grams (½ cup)
extra-virgin olive oil
6 cloves garlic, minced (about 30g)
10 salted anchovy fillets
Sea salt (if needed)**

1. Using your hand, crush the tomatoes into bite-sized pieces. Set them aside.

2. Heat the olive oil in a heavy-bottomed, sauté pan over medium heat. Add the garlic and cook for 2 minutes, or until softened. Add the anchovies and continue to cook until the garlic is browned and the anchovies have broken down.

3. Add the crushed tomatoes and cook until the sauce is slightly reduced. Raise heat to high and cook, stirring frequently, for about 10 minutes. Taste and adjust with salt (if necessary), transfer to a container, cool, and refrigerate until ready to use (up to 1 week).

béchamel sauce

Makes 1 pint (½ liter)

Béchamel is one of the five French mother sauces used to make other sauces. But it's also used in Italian cuisine (don't get the French and the Italians started on who invented what). It's a simple recipe that starts with a *roux* (fancy French for equal parts flour and fat cooked together). You always want to cook it long enough so it doesn't taste like flour, but depending on the dish, sometimes you want it darker or lighter.

The Italians use béchamel in Bolognese and lasagna. I was reluctant to use it on pizza. I'd cringe. It's that starch-on-starch thing. But when used correctly, it can be great, and I like it on some pizzas. Here we do butter and flour with a whisper of nutmeg to make it sing.

56 grams (2 ounces/4 tablespoons) unsalted butter

43 grams (1½ ounces) all-purpose flour

475 grams (16 ounces/2 cups) whole milk

Pinch grated nutmeg, plus more as needed

5 grams (1 teaspoon) sea salt, plus more as needed

Pinch ground black pepper, plus more as needed

1. Melt the butter in a medium saucepan over medium heat. Add the flour and whisk for 5 to 7 minutes, until the roux is light brown and smells nutty.

2. Slowly add the milk and whisk vigorously until the mixture begins to thicken. Lower the heat to low and add the nutmeg, salt, and black pepper.

3. Continue stirring until the sauce coats the back of a spoon, 6 to 8 minutes. Taste and adjust the seasoning and transfer to a container to cool until ready to use. Note: Use once cooled; should not be used on pizza while hot.

Sauces & Oils

195

bolognese sauce

Makes 1 quart (about 1 liter)

Brunoise. If you don't know the term, it means cutting your carrots, onions, and celery (or whatever veg) into tiny squares the same size. What the term does is explain, in one word, a precise cut everyone will know in an environment where there's little time to explain things. The reason you want veg brunoised is for even cooking times and so that you don't end up getting random giant chunks of one flavor or another. Sauce should be balanced.

**1 (794-gram/28-ounce)
can whole peeled tomatoes (preferably
Bianco DiNapoli), drained**

**30 grams (1 ounce/2 tablespoons)
unsalted butter**

**15 grams (1 tablespoon)
extra-virgin olive oil**

**20 grams (about ¾ ounce)
yellow onion, finely diced**

**7 grams (about ¼ ounce), carrot
finely diced**

**7 grams (about ¼ ounce) celery,
finely diced**

12 grams (about ½ ounce) sea salt

Freshly ground black pepper

**115 grams (about 4 ounces)
good-quality ground beef (chuck or
short rib brisket combo)**

84 grams (6 tablespoons) white wine

2 dried bay leaves

100 grams (½ cup) whole milk

**Pinch grated nutmeg,
plus more as needed**

1. Using an immersion blender, puree the whole peeled tomatoes and set aside.

2. In a medium heavy-bottomed pot, melt the butter in the olive oil over medium heat.

3. Add the onion and sweat until translucent, about 10 minutes. Add the carrot and celery and continue to cook for 8 to 10 minutes, until the vegetables soften. Season with salt and pepper.

4. Adjust the heat to high and add the ground beef. Cook until the beef is cooked and begins to brown. Deglaze with the white wine, add the bay leaves, and simmer until reduced by about half. Add the pureed tomatoes, turn the heat down to medium, and simmer uncovered for 20 minutes.

5. Add the milk and nutmeg, reduce the heat to low, cover, and continue to simmer for 3 hours, stirring occasionally. Taste and adjust the seasoning. Allow to cool and transfer to a container until ready to use. Refrigerate until ready to use (no more than 2 to 3 days).

roasted garlic cream

Makes 1 pint (½ liter)

I've used this recipe for a long time. I developed it when I had my French fry shop. You confit the garlic until it's soft and blend it with a little olive oil until it develops a rich, concentrated garlic cream flavor. For the fry shop, I'd fold it into mayonnaise. We do the same here but thicken with cream instead and blend it until the sauce is silky smooth. It maximizes the amount of garlic you can cram into a sauce, but by highlighting the garlic's sweetness, you eliminate the garlic punch. Talk about a flavor explosion. Roasted garlic cream would be great as a base for a mushroom or sausage pizza.

225 grams (about 8 ounces) cloves garlic (about 50), peeled and stems trimmed

220 grams (1 cup) extra-virgin olive oil (or enough to just cover the garlic)

Pinch sea salt

450 grams (2 cups) heavy cream

1. Combine the garlic and olive oil in a medium heavy-bottomed pot. Bring to a simmer over medium-low heat and lightly simmer for 30 minutes, or until the garlic is soft and golden brown. It should squish underneath a spoon.

2. Strain and reserve the garlic oil for other recipes.

3. Transfer the garlic to a food processor, add the salt, and blend until silky. Allow the puree to cool for about 20 minutes, then blend in the cream. The mixture should thicken but not whip. Taste and adjust the seasoning, transfer to a container, and refrigerate until ready to use (up to 1 week).

tomatillo sauce

Makes 1 quart (about 1 liter)

Tomatillo sauce is a staple of Mexican cuisine and synonymous with enchiladas, but it's great with eggs, breakfast tacos, and chilaquiles for breakfast (or any time of day), or with sour cream on potatoes that roasted in the oven. You can use it on anything, including . . . pizza.

8 green tomatillos, trimmed and halved
1 yellow onion, halved
2 jalapeños, halved
1 poblano pepper
A sprinkle of sea salt
2 cloves garlic, peeled
1 bunch cilantro, trimmed
Juice of 2 limes
40 grams (3 tablespoons) extra-virgin olive oil plus more for the baking sheet

1. Set the broiler to high. Oil a baking sheet.

2. Arrange the tomatillos, onion, and jalapeño halves and whole poblano pepper on the oiled baking sheet. Sprinkle with sea salt and broil for 5 to 8 minutes, until the skins begin to blacken. Remove from the oven.

3. Immediately remove the poblano and place it in a covered container to sweat for 2 to 5 minutes (to loosen the skin and make it easier to peel). Peel and discard the skin and seeds.

4. Combine the roasted tomatillos, onion, jalapeños, poblano, garlic, cilantro, and lime juice in a blender. Blend for 30 seconds, then slowly drizzle in the olive oil. Taste and adjust the seasoning, transfer to a container, and refrigerate until ready to use (up to 5 days).

pineapple sauce

Makes about 1 quart (about 1 liter)

When I started smoking weed, dipping things in ranch suddenly made sense. But I guess I was never high enough to unlock the code of pineapple on pizza. The inspiration for *this* pineapple sauce came from Cosme, world-renowned Chef Enrique Olvera's Mexican restaurant in New York City (his Mexico City restaurant, Pujol, has been ranked one of the world's best). Olvera's take on al pastor involves fish instead of pork, *tataki cobia* (tataki is a Japanese technique where the fish is seared but raw inside) cooked with chile and served with a smooth, velvety pineapple puree you spread onto beautiful fresh corn tortillas. I have no idea how they make their puree so good, but it made me want to make my own.

1 whole pineapple
Drizzle of neutral oil
Pinch salt

1. Preheat the oven to 450°F (232°C).

2. Cut off the crown of the pineapple and discard.

3. Line a baking sheet with heavy aluminum foil, add a small amount of oil, and bake the whole pineapple for 2 hours, or until tender throughout. Remove the pineapple and let it cool for at least 30 minutes.

4. Slice off the outside skin of the pineapple, then cut out and discard the core.

5. Cut the remaining pieces into chunks, transfer to a blender, and puree until smooth. Transfer to a saucepan and reduce on medium-low heat for about 20 minutes, until the sauce thickens.

6. Allow to cool and transfer to a squeeze bottle. Refrigerate until ready to use (no more than 2 to 3 days).

white wine lemon cream sauce

Makes 1 quart (about 1 liter)

My shrimp scampi pizza didn't set the world on fire in South Carolina, but with the leftover ingredients, I made a pizza with the White Wine Lemon Cream (WWLC) as a base, with roasted mushrooms. There's an overlap of flavors that works with mushrooms, garlic, lemon, parsley, mozzarella, Parm, and sometimes Gorgonzola, which makes this a familiar but new flavor roller-coaster. I expected a pizza using the WWLC to be a hit, but it was this afterthought pizza I threw together that became the blockbuster. WWLC is versatile for other dishes too. Pasta, obviously—clearly, shrimp scampi, but for mushroom pasta, lobster, and chicken too. It's kind of like a *beurre blanc* with lots of lemon zest and cream.

30 grams (1 ounce/2 tablespoons) unsalted butter, cubed

3 cloves garlic, minced

1 small shallot, minced

240 grams (1 cup) white wine

120 grams (½ cup) white wine vinegar

880 grams (32 ounces or 1 quart) heavy cream

Zest of 4 lemons

5 grams (1 teaspoon) sea salt

1. In a medium heavy-bottomed saucepan, melt 5 grams of the butter (about 1 teaspoon) over medium heat.

2. Add the garlic and shallot and sweat until soft and aromatic, about 4 minutes. Reduce the heat if any browning occurs.

3. Add the white wine and increase the heat to medium high. Reduce by half. Add the vinegar and reduce by half again. Stir in the cream, lemon zest, and salt. Continue to reduce until the sauce thickens and coats the back of a spoon. Whisk in the remaining butter until the sauce is homogeneous.

4. Strain, taste, and adjust the seasoning. Transfer to a container to cool until ready to use. Refrigerate until ready to use (no more than 2 to 3 days).

ranch dressing

Makes 1 pint (½ liter)

I developed this recipe over time. Occasionally I'd work with another Texan and we'd trade notes. I've settled on sour cream, chives, and garlic as the main characters. It's important to never let dill take over. The sour cream lends coolness—you get a creamy, cool, slightly tangy texture that the herbs float around in. It's best after sitting in the fridge overnight.

300 grams (1½ cups) mayonnaise

150 grams (¾ cup) buttermilk

240 grams (1 cup) sour cream

**5 grams (about ¼ ounce)
flat-leaf parsley, chopped**

1 gram dill, chopped (¾ teaspoon)

1 gram (½ teaspoon) onion powder

1 gram (½ teaspoon) garlic powder

**5 grams chives (about ¼ ounce),
chopped**

**5 grams (about ⅙ ounce) fresh garlic,
grated or finely minced**

**16 grams (about ½ ounce) fresh onion,
grated or finely minced**

**4 grams (2 teaspoons) freshly ground
black pepper**

10 grams (1½ teaspoon) sea salt

**28 grams (about 2 tablespoons)
lemon juice**

1. In a large bowl, combine all the ingredients. Taste and adjust the seasoning, transfer to a container, and refrigerate for at least 6 hours or until ready to use. Will keep for 5 to 7 days in the fridge.

2. Dip and let the haters hate.

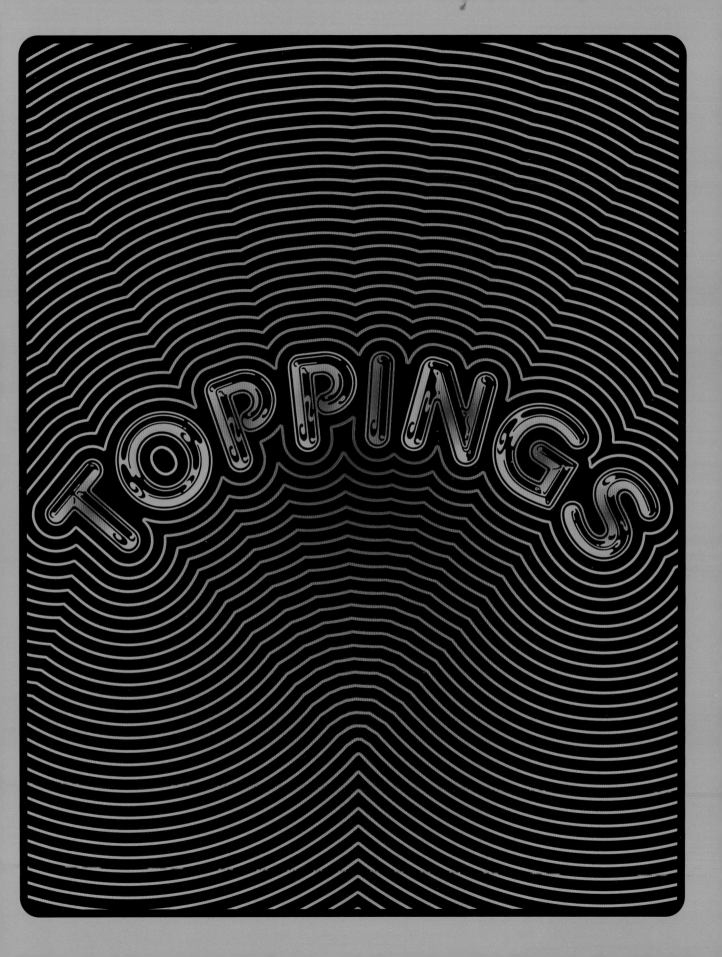

al pastor pork

Makes 1 quart (about 1 liter)

I developed this recipe with Chef Jonathan Kaldas in Charleston, South Carolina, when I was there doing a pop-up for my client Uptown Social. I had used the pineapple puree on a pizza at General Assembly in Toronto with chili-rubbed bacon, which was delicious, but not with a traditional al pastor pork—those bright red strips of sizzling pork that come flying off the *trompo* (those slow-spinning vertical rotisseries cooking over charcoal or gas flame) at taquerias. For a straight-up al pastor pie, you need proper al pastor pork—shoulder marinated in toasted chiles and pineapple juice. That's this.

450 grams (1 pound) pork shoulder
8 grams (20) dried árbol chiles,
stemmed and seeded
8 grams (1 to 2) dried guajillo chiles,
stemmed and seeded
300 grams (1¼ cups) pineapple juice
30 grams (1 ounce) achiote paste
10 grams garlic (3 cloves), peeled
5 grams (2 teaspoons) ground cumin
12 grams (2 teaspoons) kosher salt

1. Cut the pork shoulder into ½-inch (12-mm) cubes or strips. Transfer to a container with a lid and set aside.

2. In a medium cast-iron skillet over high heat, toast the chiles until they begin to blister and soften, about 5 minutes. Pour 240 ml (1 cup) water onto the chiles and remove from the heat. Set aside and allow to soak for 15 minutes.

3. In a blender, combine the drained soaked chiles, pineapple juice, achiote paste, garlic, cumin, and salt and blend until smooth. Pour the marinade over the pork, mix well, cover, and refrigerate for 24 to 48 hours.

4. Preheat the oven to 475°F (246°C).

5. Drain the pork and discard the remaining marinade. Arrange in one layer on a baking sheet and bake for 5 to 10 minutes, until the largest pieces are cooked through completely. Cool, then transfer to a container and refrigerate until ready to use. Will keep for 2 to 3 days in the fridge.

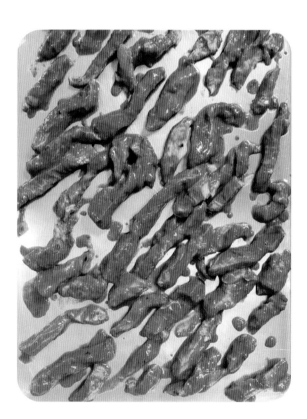

caramelized onions

Makes 1 pint (½ liter)

Caramelized onions are the equivalent of bacon for vegetarians. They add savoriness, sweetness, texture, and visual appeal. They're a great pizza topping (see pages 124 and 165). But don't believe what anyone else tells you: They take forever, require huge amounts of onions to reduce down to nothing, and they're a pain. But hey, this entire book is filled with pain-in-the-ass recipes and methods. Sometimes stuff is time-consuming. Luckily, these onions don't require tons of oversight and you can prep other things or chill while they reduce and develop flavor.

**40 grams (1½ ounces/3 tablespoons)
unsalted butter**
6 yellow onions (900 g), thinly sliced
15 grams (2¼ teaspoons) sea salt
**19 grams (1 tablespoon)
white wine vinegar**

1. In a large heavy-bottomed sauté pan, melt the butter over medium-low heat. Add the onions and salt. Cook, stirring every few minutes, for at least 1 hour, until the onions are very deep in color. If the onions start to dry out too much or stick, add some water. Keep in mind that this process is very slow and could take up to 2 hours.

2. When the onions are translucent and brown, add the vinegar. Taste and adjust the seasoning, transfer to a container, cool, and refrigerate until ready to use (up to 5 days).

lime-pickled onions

Makes 1 pint (½ liter)

This is a cool, simple Mexican technique. It's just lime juice and water. You cover the onions with the solution and they turn beautiful bright pink. It's a classic garnish for shrimp or carnitas tacos. They were added to the *cochinita pibil*–topped *panuchos* (tortillas stuffed with refried black beans) I had in Mexico City, and it was beautiful. These lime-pickled onions will be good on any pizza that you're looking to add texture, color, acid, and crunch to. Many pizzas could use that.

1 red onion, thinly sliced
Juice of 2 limes
12 grams (2 teaspoons) sea salt
473 grams (2 cups) water

1. Combine the onion, lime juice, water, and salt in a container and add just enough water to fully cover the onion.

2. Cover and refrigerate for 6 to 48 hours.

3. Drain and refrigerate until ready to use. Will keep for about 5 days in the fridge.

fingerling potatoes

Makes 6-10 potatoes

I've done fingerlings a bunch of ways on pizza. Roasted with olive oil and salt, smashed and fried, and boiled then thinly sliced. I recommend playing with those methods, and if there's another way to use potatoes you come across or come up with that's *not* in this book, try that too.

Handful of fingerling potatoes
Handful of sea salt

4. Put the potatoes in a large pot and cover with cold water. Season generously with salt and bring to a boil.

5. Boil potatoes until fork tender, 10 to 20 minutes depending on the size.

falco sausage

Makes 900 grams (2 pounds)

The longer I make this recipe, the more things get added. A few years back, I was prepping at Ava Gene's in Portland, Oregon, with Chef Joshua McFadden, who I was doing a pop-up with at Feast Portland. They add white wine to their sausage. I thought that was cool because of the flavor and moisture it brings—along with a touch of class—so I do that too.

My original sausage recipe was simple: fennel, salt, chile flakes, and black pepper. That's the basis of good Italian-style pork sausage (fennel is number one). Sugar is something I rarely use, but it adds color to the cooked sausage and that sweetness accents the fat and spices. Don't want to use sugar? Fine.

12 grams (2 teaspoons) sea salt

4 grams (1½ teaspoons) black peppercorns

6 grams (2½ teaspoons) fennel seeds

8 grams (2 teaspoons) brown sugar

Pinch dried Calabrian chile flakes

900 grams (2 pounds) ground pork (high-quality heritage pork)

2 cloves garlic, minced

15 grams (1 tablespoon) white wine (drink some to make sure it's good)

5 grams (1 teaspoon) extra-virgin olive oil

1. Combine the salt, black peppercorns, fennel seeds, and brown sugar in a spice grinder or using a mortar and pestle and grind until fine.

2. In a large bowl, combine the ground pork, spice mixture, garlic, white wine, and olive oil. Mix quickly and carefully until just combined. Transfer to a container and refrigerate until ready to use. Will keep for 2 to 3 days in the fridge.

3. Optional but recommended: In a small skillet over medium-high heat, sear a coin sized chunk of the sausage mixture in a little olive oil. Once cooked through, taste and adjust the seasoning of the sausage mixture accordingly.

Toppings

fried garlic chips

Makes 1 pint (½ liter)

These are a great addition to *all kinds* of pizzas. They're also great on garlic bread, tossed in or as garnish for pasta, and as a finishing touch on top of roasted broccoli. They have great texture and crunch. Just make and use them fresh. They die after a few days. Always add them after the pizza comes out of the oven.

275 grams (1¼ cups) vegetable oil
500 grams (25 cloves) garlic,
sliced extremely thin on a
Japanese mandoline
1 gram (a pinch) sea salt

1. Heat the vegetable oil in a sauté pan over medium-high heat until the oil begins to shimmer. Add the sliced garlic and fry, stirring constantly, for 5 minutes or until light golden brown. Using a mesh strainer, drain the garlic from the hot oil.

2. Transfer the garlic chips to a tray lined with a double layering of paper towel. Season with the salt. The chips will last about 5 days at room temperature sitting on paper towels inside a container with a tightly fitting lid.

fried eggplant cutlets

Makes 6 cutlets

Fried eggplant cutlets are great on pizza. You could do a straightforward eggplant Parm pizza like the one on page 185, where you throw down the cutlets, place the sauce and mozzarella on them, bake it, top it with basil and Parmigiano-Reggiano, and call it a day. You could also bake these cutlets in the oven, layered like lasagna with mozzarella and tomato sauce and Parm and serve it with pasta or on its own with broccoli rabe and it would be amazing.

125 grams (8 ounces) all-purpose flour

18 grams (1 tablespoon) sea salt, plus more for finishing

6 grams (2 teaspoons) freshly ground black pepper

6 grams (2 teaspoons) dried Calabrian chile flakes

4 eggs

100 grams (about 3½ ounces) Sourdough Breadcrumbs (page 226)

50 grams (about 1¾ ounces) Parmigiano-Reggiano, grated

20 grams (about ¾ ounce) flat-leaf parsley, chopped

1 liter (1 quart) extra-virgin olive oil

2 medium Italian eggplants

Large pinch dried wild Sicilian oregano, stems removed

1. Set up 3 shallow pans or low-sided bowls in succession. Combine the flour, 10 grams (1½ teaspoons) of the salt, the black pepper, and the chile flakes in the first bowl. In the second bowl, combine the eggs with a splash of water and whisk to combine. In the last bowl, combine the breadcrumbs, Parmigiano-Reggiano, parsley, and the remaining sea salt.

2. In a large, heavy-bottomed pot such as enameled cast-iron, heat the blended olive oil over medium heat until it reads 375°F (190°C) on a candy thermometer.

3. Remove the crown of the eggplants, and with a vegetable peeler, remove the skin. Do this step last to avoid oxidation (browning). Cut lengthwise into 1-inch- (2½-cm-) thick cutlets.

4. Working one cutlet at a time, dredge in the flour, coating thoroughly and then shaking to remove any excess flour. Transfer to the egg, then to the breadcrumb mixture, pressing to make the breadcrumbs adhere. Transfer the eggplant pieces to a resting rack or paper towels to let them dry slightly before frying. Repeat with the remaining cutlets.

5. Fry the cutlets in small batches, making sure not to crowd the pot, for 3 to 5 minutes total (can turn halfway through), until golden brown. Transfer to a resting rack with a paper towel beneath and season the cutlets with salt. Let cool.

lamb sausage

Makes 1 pint (½ liter)

This is a versatile recipe that requires a lot of spices. Just be careful with the cinnamon—too much can easily overpower the blend of flavors. If you get it right, it's fantastic. Start with the best ground lamb you can find and keep an open mind as to what to use this blend for. It goes great on pizza, sure, but it would make a great burger, and one time, I mixed leftover sausage, onions, tomato sauce, labneh, mint, and parsley to create a sauce for one of the best pastas I've ever made.

6 grams (1 teaspoon) kosher salt
3 grams (1 teaspoon) paprika
3 grams (1 teaspoon) ground cumin
3 grams (1 teaspoon) ground coriander
3 grams (1 teaspoon) garlic powder
2 grams (1 teaspoon) fennel seeds
1 gram (½ teaspoon) ground cinnamon
½ gram (1 teaspoon) dried thyme
230 grams (8 ounces) ground lamb

1. Combine the salt, paprika, cumin, coriander, garlic powder, fennel seeds, cinnamon, and thyme in a spice grinder or using mortar and pestle and grind until fine.

2. In a large bowl, combine the lamb with the spice mixture. Using your hands, mix the sausage until just combined. In a small skillet over medium-high heat, sear a coin sized chunk of the sausage mixture in a little olive oil. Once cooked through, taste and adjust the sausage mixture accordingly.

3. Transfer to a container and refrigerate until ready to use. Will keep for 2 to 3 days in the fridge.

How to Use a Japanese Mandoline without Cutting Yourself

The old widow-maker. That's what the Japanese mandoline is called in the kitchen. I'm kidding, but seriously, it's dangerous. It's compact, portable, effective, reasonably priced, and resilient, which is why you'll find this handy tool in professional kitchens everywhere. Ideally, using one should be faster than a knife, but even if not, you'll end up with beautifully sliced veg. It's also incredibly sharp and deadly. Have Band-Aids on hand.

Go slow. That's key. You could also wear two gloves on the slicing hand so if you hit the blade, it will snag the glove, or not cut you quite as badly. Do not be a hero. You are not impressing anyone. I'm impressed if you don't cut yourself. If you do want to go fast (you will), start brave when you have lots left of whatever you're slicing, then slow down at the last third. Remember, it's a slippery slope.

I've never told someone using a mandoline to go faster. Nor will I ever. Take. Your. Time.

marinated shrimp

Makes 1 cup (60 ml)

I bought a bunch of spices, salts, and seasonings from this amazing chile store in Kyoto while I was on an R&D trip in Japan to check out Tokyo-style pizza. The spices were beautifully packaged and tasted amazing. *Yuzu kosho*, a fermented Japanese chile paste, is especially fun. It's salty and spicy, with a fruity fermented flavor that pairs with anything and is especially great in shrimp marinade.

Speaking of which, always buy wild-caught frozen shrimp. Unless you live in Louisiana or Charleston, South Carolina, it's likely that the "fresh" shrimp on ice in your local supermarket was frozen, defrosted, and iced to make it look sexy to sell it. Skip the middleman, support shrimp fishermen, and buy the stuff frozen on the boat. Farmed shrimp doesn't taste as good and can be destructive to the environment. When you've had delicious fresh-caught shrimp, there's nothing like it.

10 grams (1 teaspoon) yuzu kosho
Zest and juice of 1 lemon
1 clove garlic, minced
**20 grams (1½ tablespoons)
extra-virgin olive oil**
**350 grams (about 12 ounces)
frozen wild-caught shrimp, thawed,
peeled, deveined, and cut into
nickel-sized pieces**

1. In a container with a lid, combine the yuzu kosho, lemon zest and juice, garlic, and olive oil. Whisk quickly to break up any chunks.

2. Add the shrimp and toss gently in the marinade. Cover and refrigerate for at least 1 hour but preferably between 12 to 24 hours before using.

mashed potatoes

Makes 1 quart (about 1 liter)

If you're going to put mashed potatoes on pizza, they should be really good. This is a recipe for really good mashed potatoes. It's also an example of how executing little things well can almost be more important than measurements. For instance, boiling potatoes for the right time—not so short they're still raw, and not too long they're falling apart—you want to hit that sweet spot where they're fork-tender and you drain and air-dry them. Using a ricer, or a masher if you don't have one, is important. For this recipe, a touch of nutmeg and garlic is nice for subtle background notes, along with lots of freshly ground black pepper. These are delicious on their own. But also, be a crazy person and put them on pizza.

**4 Yukon Gold potatoes,
peeled and cubed**

**20 grams (1 tablespoon) sea salt,
plus more for the water**

50 grams (1¾ ounces) unsalted butter

1 clove garlic, minced

240 grams (1 cup) heavy cream

Pinch ground nutmeg

1. Put the potatoes in a large pot and cover with cold water. Season generously with salt and bring to a boil. Cook until a fork slides easily into the largest cube (about 15 to 20 minutes depending on size of potatoes). Drain well and allow them to dry on a sheet pan in one layer.

2. Meanwhile, in a small saucepan, melt the butter over medium-low heat. Add the garlic and cook until soft, about 5 minutes. Add the cream and nutmeg.

3. While the potatoes are still hot, mash or rice them (preferred) in a large bowl. Pour the warm cream and butter mixture into the mashed potatoes, season with the salt, and mix until the cream mixture is fully combined and the mashed potatoes are smooth. Taste and adjust the seasoning. Cool, then transfer to a piping bag and refrigerate until use. Will keep for 2 to 3 days in the fridge.

roasted brussels sprouts

Makes 1 pint (½ liter)

One of my earliest food memories was at the dining room table by myself because I refused my Brussels sprouts. I forced one down then covered them in the garbage. I was trying to be smart, so I left a piece on the plate, let time pass, and was like, "I'm done!" My dad came in, looked at the plate then me, and immediately I realized I was in trouble. He *knew*. Butter was sliding off the side of the plate and suddenly I understood the man I was dealing with and that I'd never get anything by him.

Now, if my parents had done a better job cooking sprouts, we wouldn't have been in that boiled, pale green–flavored, steamed situation. And it's a shame because Brussels sprouts can be delicious. They had a trendy moment in the aughts when they were on the menu of every restaurant I cooked at. People finally figured them out: a nice thick kosher salt, good olive oil, and high heat.

There's not much to it. Just cook them as quickly as possible. Rage your oven as high as it will go and throw them in on a sheet pan until the tops start to blacken (halving them cooks them faster). They turn a nice bright green where they're not browned or charred. Taste the smallest one—it should have crunch and the char should be sweet. Take them off the hot pan so it doesn't continue cooking them, but don't bunch them while they're hot or they'll steam each other. From there they'll make a fantastic pizza topping. You can also shred them with a mandoline, toss them with salt and olive oil, and again, roast them using super high heat, like a minute in a 500°F (260°C) oven. By the way, this works for everything in the brassica family: broccoli, Broccolini, kale, cauliflower, bok choy, collards, cabbage. You'll never look at any of them, but especially Brussels sprouts, the same way.

453 grams (1 pound) Brussels sprouts, washed, trimmed, and thinly sliced lengthwise (preferably on a Japanese mandoline; see page 216)

25 grams (1½ tablespoons) extra-virgin olive oil

10 grams (1½ teaspoons) sea salt, plus more as needed

Pinch freshly ground black pepper

1. Preheat the oven to 500°F (260°C).

2. On a half sheet pan, lay out the sliced Brussels sprouts in a thin, even layer. Drizzle with the olive oil, sprinkle with the salt, toss to combine, and redistribute them in a thin, even layer.

3. Roast for 2 to 5 minutes, until the leaves just begin to brown (they should remain mostly al dente). Transfer to another tray and allow to cool.

4. Season with the black pepper, taste, and adjust the salt to taste. Refrigerate until ready to use (no more than 2 to 3 days).

Wild Sicilian Oregano

You can use other oregano, but wild Sicilian oregano—it's a different variety with sweet and spicy notes and a more floral aroma. Do yourself a favor and get some wild Sicilian oregano on the stem, trust me.

sicilian onion topping

Makes ½ cup (30 ml)

This is all the best flavors of Sicily in one pizza topping. Put this on the Sicilian dough and you'll have a delicious Sicilian pizza, focaccia, grandma pie, or whatever you want to call it. And it's easy. Sicilian anchovy fillets (a classic pantry staple of Sicilian food), onions (plentiful and cheap), breadcrumbs (from our sourdough breadcrumbs; page 226), some *really* good olive oil, garlic, and, crucially, wild Sicilian oregano.

40 grams (3 tablespoons)
extra virgin olive oil

3 cloves garlic, minced

20 grams Sicilian anchovy fillets
(5 fillets), deboned and minced

110 grams (about 4 ounces)
yellow onion, sliced

Sea salt

Pinch dried wild Sicilian oregano,
stems removed

20 grams (about ¾ ounce)
Sourdough Breadcrumbs (page 226)

1. Heat 30 grams (about 2½ tablespoons) of the olive oil in a sauté pan over medium heat. Add the garlic and cook until softened but not browned, 1 to 2 minutes. Add the anchovies and cook until they begin to break down, about 1 minute. Add the onion, season with salt, and cook until the onion begins to soften, 10 to 15 minutes. Add the breadcrumbs, oregano, and the remaining olive oil, stir to combine, and remove the pan from the heat.

2. Allow to cool, then transfer to a small container and refrigerate until ready to use (no more than 2 to 3 days).

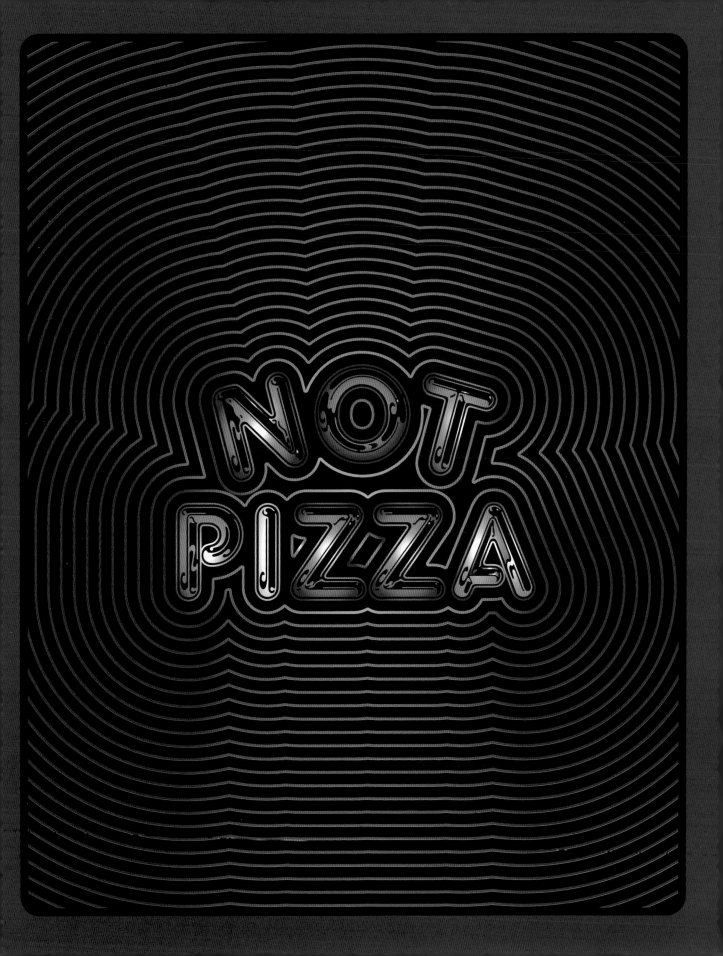

MEATBALLS

Talk with any Italian-American and they'll tell you about their family's meatballs. I'm no different. I grew up in a Sicilian-American family, and I'm going to share my grandma's recipe for meatballs. It may seem like a standard story, but it's not. In this case, I waited thirty years to try them.

My grandma Mary was born in Louisiana and grew up in a Sicilian farming community in Highbank, Texas. She married my grandfather at a young age and they moved to nearby Marlin, Texas, where they farmed and operated Tony's Liquor, named after my grandfather.

As was common in Italian-American communities, Tony's mother, my great-grandmother Lena, lived next door. Almost all my childhood holidays and many summers were spent in Marlin, with cousins, uncles, and aunts from the combined Falco and Salvato families. My family would travel from Austin, where I grew up pretty disconnected from the Italian-American community. I grew up eating food my great-grandmother and grandma prepared at these gatherings: pizza, fresh bread, *sugo* (slow-cooked tomato sauce), *cucuzza*, fava beans, potato and squash casseroles, and veggies from Lena's garden.

But I never had my grandmother's meatballs. I saw them, along with sausages, baked eggs, and all kinds of meats, as off-limits to me. That's because my dad, in the process of moving to Austin in the '70s, became a vegetarian hippie. My great-grandmother prepared meat and vegetarian versions of everything. My dad would make vegetarian meatballs, and I never thought much about it until my twenties.

At that point, I had worked in many restaurants and cooked meat. But I never considered switching from my vegetarian upbringing until I was about to start working at a restaurant in Brooklyn dedicated to sourcing the highest-quality meats. I didn't want to be "that vegetarian cook" again. There was an upcoming holiday party at Peter Luger for the bar I worked at. What better place to lose my meat virginity than at New York City's most famous steakhouse?

I started with the famous bacon. Turns out I really liked it. I ate shrimp cocktail and steak, drinking heavily to steel my nerves. Not only did I not get sick as some predicted, I felt great. I tried everything if it was offered to me, a rule I live by with pride to this day. Then on a trip home to Texas, the moment of truth: I told my grandma I was no longer a vegetarian. She didn't skip a beat. "Oh, good," she said. "Let's go to Lockhart and get barbecue!"

The dividends of my new eating habits paid off. At Kreuz Market, I told her I was dying to try her meatballs. The next day we made them together. I was not disappointed. They were delicious. I felt like I'd claimed a long-lost birthright. Here's how they're special.

All-Beef or Mostly Beef: Grandma Mary's from Falls County, Texas: This is cattle country, where beef is king. So my grandma's meatballs were almost always all beef. If you want to use pork or veal, it shouldn't affect the recipe.

Sooooo Much Parmesan and Very Little Binder: There's a lot of cheese in this recipe. I like Parmesan and Pecorino—my grandma used both. I've added a panade (a mixture of starch and liquid), but she never used one.

"Mamma Mia, That's a Spicy Meatball!": Being Sicilians, and being Texan, spice is a part of life. The recipe makes a spicy meatball, so if you have a low tolerance for heat, bring it down a bit.

Fennel for the Win: Fennel and fennel seeds were featured prominently in many of my Sicilian-American family recipes. I like to grind fennel seeds with other spices and salt to make a blend that seasons the meat evenly without chunks of fennel seeds. If you want to go more rustic and not grind the spices, cool.

Sunday Dinner Perfection: One of the great things about this recipe for Sunday dinner is you can make these meatballs the day before and chill them overnight. They'll hold their shape better and all you have to do the next day is pop them in the oven or fry them in a pan before they take a swim in your sauce.

Tallow

Quite a few of my recipes call for meat. I think it's important (and will make these recipes even better) if you find a local whole-animal butcher. You won't find a row of pork chops perfectly shrink-wrapped, but a few along with every other part of the animal. This is the ethical way to consume meat. A pig is more than a pork chop. Pigs have ears, skin, and heads, which can be turned into head cheese. If you eat animals, it's important to know how they became food.

I'm lucky to live down the street from The Meat Hook, one of America's best whole-animal butchers. They source from local farms they've visited to see how the animals are raised, cared for, and humanely slaughtered. A whole-animal butcher needs to sell every part of the animal to make profit, so you'll see various forms of animal fat. They'll mix some in with sausages and ground meat, but inevitably there will be more fat than they can use. You'll find leaf lard (the soft fat from around the pig's loin and kidneys), chunks of pork fat, and tallow. These are great things to include in recipes.

You can doctor ground beef or pork by rendering and mixing the fat in. You can cook beans in it. You can even use it as a butter replacement in my ButterCrust Pan Pizza recipe (page 136). It's a nice thing to have in your freezer. Fat, I think, as we're better understanding how nutrition works, is actually good for you. Don't be afraid of it.

sicilian texan grandma's meatballs

Makes about 12 meatballs

I'm not going to lie: You may need to do a little work to get the right blend of fat to meat. You'll have to go to your butcher and say, "Can you grind me some 80/20?" to get that extra fat in the meat. Once you have it, instead of cooking these meatballs through (per the recipe), you can also bake them for about 20 minutes, until they're firm but rare in the center, then finish them by poaching in Robust Tomato Sauce (page 54). It will add even more flavor to the sauce. Serve them garnished with Pecorino-Romano, chopped parsley, and toasted breadcrumbs. There are few better things in life.

80 grams (2 slices) stale bread, cubed

84 grams (6 tablespoons) whole milk

6 grams (2 teaspoons) freshly ground black pepper

6 grams (2 teaspoons) dried Calabrian chile flakes

6 grams (2 teaspoons) fennel seeds

18 grams (1 tablespoon) sea salt

1 bunch flat-leaf parsley (stems removed), chopped

800 grams (1¾ pounds) ground beef (brisket–short rib blend, 20% fat)

80 grams (3 ounces) tallow, at room temperature (optional)

100 grams (3½ ounces) Parmigiano-Reggiano, finely grated

75 grams (2¾ ounces) Pecorino-Romano, finely grated

25 grams (1 ounce) Sourdough Breadcrumbs (page 226), toasted

Extra-virgin olive oil

1. Combine the bread cubes and milk in a small bowl. Let soak and set aside.

2. In a spice grinder or in a mortar with a pestle, grind the black pepper, chile flakes, fennel seeds, and salt into a fine powder.

3. In a food processor, combine the milk-soaked bread and the parsley and blend to a smooth consistency. Transfer the panade to a large bowl. Add the ground beef and tallow (if desired), the spice mixture, grated cheeses, and breadcrumbs. Using gloves, gently mix by hand until incorporated, but be sure not to overmix!

4. Roll out a very small ball, about the size of a marble, and cook it off in a frying pan. Taste it for seasoning and add extra salt or spices to your preference.

5. Line a sheet pan with parchment paper and pour some olive oil into a small bowl. Set aside.

6. Lightly oil your hands and roll the meatballs according to your size preference. I prefer them slightly larger than a golf ball. Place the meatballs on the parchment-lined sheet pan with ½ inch (12 mm) of space between them. Cover and chill for at least 1 hour.

7. Preheat the oven to 275°F (135°C).

8. Bake the meatballs for 30 minutes, or until an instant-read thermometer registers an internal temperature of 165°F (74°C). Use immediately or refrigerate for up to 3 days.

9. You can use these meatballs however you like—crumble cooled meatballs for topping a pizza or make a meatball hero.

PRODUCTS

My process when I'm consulting does *not* involve recommending brands, so I won't do that here.

I say, "These are good brands. If you like others or you're curious about ones that I've never used, let's bring those to the table too." We're going to shred it up. We're going to bake pizzas using different ingredients and determine which ingredients we like for this pizza.

That's what I recommend *you* do. Buy a few mozzarellas—whole milk, part-skim, and fresh—get some provolone and caciocavallo, get every tomato and olive oil that looks good, and put them on pizza in different blends. See what works. Do the same for every ingredient you plan to use, and take notes.

But I do have thoughts on ingredients and producers.

STONE-MILLED VERSUS ROLLER-MILLED: There are two important points about flour to understand. There's stone-milled flour and roller-milled flour. The first is what it sounds like, two stones that grind together, milling wheat berries between them. That's the ancient way. The modern way involves factory roller mills that process more flour more effectively. The problem with roller mills is the flour they produce is less nutritious. That niacin, thiamin, iron, and riboflavin on the label is added enrichment because the natural equivalent was removed—it attracts insects and spoils.

The majority of flour is roller-milled. That doesn't mean it's bad—it feeds lots of people—but if you're looking for the most nutritious flour, incorporate freshly milled whole grains. They add flavor to dough and you can blend them with white flours for great results.

Stone milling is making a comeback. I've visited mills and used many freshly milled flours. Cairnspring Mills in Washington State's Skagit Valley makes two that I love, Skagit 1109 and Edison. Camas Country Mill does great flour out of Eugene, Oregon. Barton Springs Mill, twenty minutes west of Austin, Texas, is new but good.

I'm not saying you have to use any of those—the idea is to try something different. Try stone-milled heritage wheat and see what happens. If you don't like it, go back to the supermarket. Over the years, I've become interested in unique products. Once you start playing with them, you may too.

ITALIAN 00 FLOUR: Its mythical status has faded, but I frequently get asked about double zero flour. It's not enriched, and if it's coming from Italy, it's never bleached or bromated. It performs great for wood fire–cooked dough but works for other styles too. It's silky smooth because "00" means it's finely milled with an ash content of 0.55%, extraction of 50%, and a protein content minimum of 9%. Italians usually use soft wheat, durum, or semolina—00 pizza flour is soft wheat. Other countries have different corresponding milling specs. So Italian 00 flour closely matches T45 French flour, 405 German flour, and in America, pastry flour.

Why Doesn't Everyone Go Natural?

It's difficult. You have to maintain a starter. You have to feed it. If you go on vacation, you have to store it and wake it again or get someone to feed it. That's out of line with convenience culture. But when places like Tartine in San Francisco started doing this, it spoke to people looking for something ancient and simple. My opinion? When people taste pizza with higher-quality flour and better quality of fermentation, a light turns on. "More of *this*."

TYPES OF WHEAT

Wheat has been cultivated for over ten thousand years. There are thousands of varieties, possibly a dozen or more different species, ranging from small pockets of wild wheat or ancient grains to the world's most cultivated cereal crop, common wheat. As I've traveled, my understanding of varieties that go into the flour I'm using is the beginning. Acquiring a small tabletop mill has allowed me to incorporate varieties of wheat berries into my doughs. I'll think about different varieties in the initial stages of considering the dough I want. A tender and puffy Neapolitan-style pizza cooked in a high-temperature oven may best be achieved with a soft white wheat. A hard red spring wheat would be a starting point for a crispy and chewy New York–style pizza. I almost always blend to achieve flavors and textures unachievable from just one type. More often than not, flour types will *include* a blend, like a bread flour or an all-purpose flour.

WINTER WHEAT: Winter wheat is planted in fall and needs cold temperatures to go through the process of vernalization over winter, which is what allows it to go into seed production in the spring.

SPRING WHEAT: Planted in the spring and harvested in late summer or fall. High-protein wheats are generally spring wheat, like durum wheat.

WHEATS

DURUM: Durum is a high-protein wheat used to make semolina flour. I've used semolina in pizza dough at percentages ranging from 2% to 10% to add flavor and crispiness. Its flavor and texture can dominate a soft white or hard red wheat.

HARD RED SPRING: You'll find this in high-protein bread flours. I use it for my Thin & Crispy and New York–style pizzas. It's also good for pan pies. It's often used in bread flours because of its high gluten content. Canada produces and exports tons of it.

HARD RED WINTER: The most widely grown wheat in America. It's planted in the fall and harvested in spring or early summer, from Texas to North Dakota, and used in all-purpose flours.

SOFT RED WINTER: Mostly used for pastry flour. It can be used for pizza but it's not as widely used in pizza making as the soft white used in 00 flour.

HARD WHITE: Found in all-purpose flours and sometimes white whole wheat. Not something pizza people use de rigueur.

SOFT WHITE: It's planted as both "winter" and "spring" wheat, but that's generally not specified. Regardless, it's used in 00 flours and moderate-protein flours that add extensibility and tenderness. I've also used a heritage variety called Sonora White—the first variety of wheat introduced to the New World.

TOMATOES:
CANNED OR FRESH,
AND
HOW TO PICK THE
RIGHT BRAND

Canned. Fresh tomatoes grown green and gassed or hydroponic tomatoes will never have the flavor of vine-ripened tomatoes. If you have in-season cherry tomatoes, halve and dress them with salt and olive oil, and put them on a pizza with garlic, mozzarella, basil, and Parm. The fresh tomatoes shine. But that's a seasonal thing and the season is short. The rest of the time, sauce should come from canned tomatoes.

When I'm making pizza in North America, I'm using tomatoes from California or New Jersey. I've had great experiences with Stanislaus and Bianco DiNapoli Tomatoes (Bianco is Chris Bianco of Pizzeria Bianco in Arizona, one of America's most famous pizzerias).

I *love* Stanislaus. Based out of Stanislaus County, California, the company was founded in 1942 by the Quartaroli family and eventually bought by the Cortopassi family in 1978. I've toured their facilities—their dedication to quality is borderline psychotic, which I relate to. They only pack perfectly ripened tomatoes. It's unique in the industry and something that makes them special. The problem is they can be difficult to find in stores. Their whole peeled tomato product is called Alta Cucina. It comes in a #10 can, industry speak for a commonly used can size in the wholesale world (it holds nearly seven pounds).

If you want a more American, cooked-down flavor, Stanislaus makes Saporito Filetto di Pomodoro ("strips of peeled tomato"). And their Tomato Magic is great for Thin & Crispy Pizza. It's a chunky, meatier sauce made with ground peeled tomatoes that are slightly sweet. It's great for reinforcing other sauces with nuanced extra flavor people won't be able single out. Bianco DiNapoli tomatoes are great (also organic)—produced down the road from Stanislaus and you can find them everywhere.

I also like Fattoria Fresca Jersey Fresh whole peeled and crushed with basil (no citric acid). I use them for home recipes. They tend to be available more around the East Coast.

Outside North America, I almost exclusively use Italian tomatoes. But when I start a pizza program, we investigate every canned tomato available in that area, either from a distributor or a cash and carry (a wholesale warehouse that operates on a self-service basis). We read labels, determine if it's just tomatoes and citric acid, or if it's tomatoes, citric acid, calcium chloride, and salt, and whether there's basil.

If there are additions, we'll account for that while tasting, but we're still tasting them all. If they're whole peeled, we'll drain them first, and if they're chopped, we'll just dig in. We decide what tastes best, then look at prices. Hopefully the best ones are realistically priced. That's it. I don't guarantee you'll love certain brands. But it's important to have the vocabulary to discuss what you're tasting. You're looking for bitter, sweet, acidic, and savory.

PIZZA CHEESES

There's aged mozzarella and fresh mozzarella, and then in the fresh mozz category, there's buffalo and *fior di latte* cow mozzarella. Anywhere I go I want the best cheese, locally.

Aged mozzarella is crucial for New York–style pizza, and Grande is the industry leader. It's widespread because it doesn't break as easily. One of the challenges with New York–style versus wood-fired pizza is when you're making a wood-fired pizza, your pizza is in a 900°F (482°C) oven for 90 seconds or less and the fresh mozzarella barely melts. The lower temperature of gas ovens (600°F/315°C or less) and longer bake tends to overcook fresh mozzarella, breaking and turning it greasy and chewy. There's lots to be said for greasy pizza, but there's a limit.

Buying buffalo mozzarella from Italy is expensive in the States and can be extraordinarily delicious or mediocre. Yes, you can find great dairy on the East and West Coasts, but dairy production is centered in the Midwest. If someone local does great fresh mozzarella, use them. Just use the best product.

If you're making mozz (see page 40), a hot water process called *pasta filata* (a stretched curd method of making fresh cheese), you need curd. Curd can be tough to find outside the East Coast. I usually use BelGioioso. They're family-owned and they use quality milk. Polly-O is good, just owned by a behemoth corporation (Kraft). I've used curd from Narragansett Creamery (Rhode Island) and Lioni Latticini out of Brooklyn and New Jersey—both very good.

I recommend trying other cheeses. There are special cheeses intended to be eaten raw, cold, or room temperature, and it would be a shame to put them on pizza. They also tend to be expensive and lose subtleties in the oven. Eliminate them.

I look for good finishing cheeses, but with pizza cheese, I want something that melts well, has good flavor, and isn't expensive. Cheese is already one of the highest pizza food costs, so don't go overboard.

When I started making pizza and needed cheese ideas, I'd talk to cheesemongers and check out regional cheeses at Murray's in the West Village. That's how I came across The Cellars at Jasper Hill in Vermont. They make a great Cheddar called Chef Shreds. Another fantastic pizza cheese from Vermont is Spring Brook Farm Tarentaise by Thistle Hill Farm. Milton Creamery out of Iowa makes a cave-aged Cheddar called Prairie Breeze that's an amazing pizza cheese. Cascadia Creamery in the Pacific Northwest does Sawtooth. Funky, creamy, and similar to Taleggio, when mixed with mozzarella, it makes an interesting pizza.

Try a bunch and see what works.

OLIVE OIL

I don't care what the label says, you know great olive oil when you taste it. I want it to be fruity and acidic, but not overly acidic. There should be spice, but it shouldn't burn your throat (a bad sign). Good olive oil disappears into your mouth. The best in the world comes from Sicily, but that's not always easy to find. I love Corto Olive Oil from Stanislaus, but it's hard to go wrong with most California olive oil if it's fresh.

LOCAL AND SEASONAL:

DO IT, DON'T DRONE ABOUT IT

You see it on menus all the time, "We use local/seasonal ingredients whenever possible." There's no reason to put this on your menu. One, it's ineffectual. What's your definition of "local" anyway? Also, if you say, "We *only* use local and seasonal ingredients," you'll have a *really* tough time operating with a consistent menu, especially in winter and season to season. It's a hard promise and it's wishy-washy. Why say it? Just make great pizza. The reasons you use local and seasonal ingredients are they *taste* better, it's interesting to connect with local farmers and producers, and you get to be a part of a small slow-food system.

WHAT DO MOST PIZZERIAS THAT USE COMMERCIAL YEAST DO?

The process is simple; it begins by dissolving yeast in water. Some add sugar to activate the yeast, which isn't necessary. And some use warm water, also unnecessary.

In New York City and many commercial-style pizzerias, they keep the process warm. They add half a percent or less of yeast, let it rise, then use it as fast as they can, sometimes the same day. On the other spectrum of commercial yeast, you have the Romans, who add 1 gram of yeast to a 10,000-gram batch of dough, a tiny fraction of a percentage of the flour. Then they proof for 5 days. In the middle, Neapolitans generally do a 48-hour fermentation with commercial yeast.

Sometimes people refrigerate dough to slow the commercial yeast. That's called a cold ferment and it's done to develop more flavor. Here's the rule: The less you use, the longer you can ferment, and if you put it in a cold area, it will extend fermentation.

NATURAL FERMENTATION—
WHAT THE HELL IS THAT?

Sourdough can be controversial. It shouldn't be. It's the way bread was leavened for millennia. It was only in the nineteenth century that systems were invented to mass-produce yeast. Before that, we used a byproduct of beer-making yeast to make bread. *All* bread was naturally leavened.

By that I mean yeast and bacteria harvested naturally and used to ferment dough (and make bread rise by producing carbon dioxide). If you mix flour and water, eventually bacteria and yeast colonize it. Once it settles, you have a stable colony called a SCOBY (symbiotic culture of bacteria and yeast). That's how bread's been made forever.

When commercial yeast was introduced, people liked its convenience and reliability, but not necessarily its flavor. Techniques like *poolish* (a wet yeast-cultured dough used in French bakery products, one part flour to one part water) and *biga* (a drier Italian poolish, usually two parts flour, one part water) were developed to coax flavor out of bread made with commercial yeast.

So what's the big deal? Some people take issue with it not being "traditional" to use sourdough in pizza. Others get bent out of shape about applying bread-making techniques to pizza: "Pizza is not bread."

The lifespan of pizza as we know it has mostly existed within the realm of commercial yeast, but no one knows when the first pizzas were made, if they were naturally leavened or made with commercial yeast.

I'd guess natural leavening because pizza started being made when commercial yeast was just becoming available.

As far as pizza in New York City, I'd guess most was made with commercial yeast going back to its origins. Does that make it traditional? And what do the Italians say? VPN (Vera Pizza Napoletana) Americas, the American delegation of the Italian nonprofit that established the "rules" of Neapolitan pizza in the '80s, says, "Compressed yeast, biologically produced, solid, soft and beige in color, with quite an insipid taste and a low degree of acidity, must be used."

They also say: "The crust should deliver the flavor of well-prepared, baked bread."

There you go, straight from the mouth of the Italian authorities. Pizza should have the flavor of bread. Know what else they say? "Use of natural yeast is also permitted."

Here's my take. If you think someone's wrong for using commercial yeast or natural leavening, *you're* wrong. There's no *wrong thing*. It's preference. I prefer low-acidic dough. As far as rule-makers go, so does the VPN.

In New York City, the self-proclaimed and generally regarded pizza capital of America, crust has been an afterthought. Many pizzerias held up as greats use flat-tasting doughs. People who defend that say too much crust flavor distracts. I *want* flavor depth. People just get stuck in their ways.

Know what, though? Many are coming around to natural fermentation. That's fun.

The Greats of Natural Leavening

Anthony Mangieri has done naturally leavened pizza longer and with more dedication and conviction than anyone. He's an inspiration. When I started making pizza I lived in the East Village, where he had his first New York City pizzeria, Una Pizza Napoletana. I couldn't afford it often, but it was great. There wasn't anywhere near the amount of Neapolitan or wood-fired pizza available then. We've become friends, and one thing we love about natural leavening is the challenge and fun of it. Since Anthony, many have done natural leavening, among them Sarah Minnick of Lovely's Fifty Fifty and Scott Rivera of Scottie's Pizza Parlor, both in Portland, Oregon. If you haven't tried these pizzerias, get to them.

Making Natural Leavening, aka Sourdough, aka Levain, aka Starter, aka Magic

When making naturally leavened pizza, leavener can be referred to as sourdough, levain, starter, and preferment. People use the terms for different things. With levain, you probably mean sourdough starter (it's a French baking word). Sourdough means the same thing, but some people who aren't trying to make a sour product don't like to use it. I refer to mine as a starter, but some people refer to bigas or poolishes as starters too. People even name their starters. At Upside in Times Square, which I consulted on, they named theirs "Tibby." ("It just felt right," partner Noam Grossman said.)

There are all different kinds of yeast. Baker's yeast is *Saccharomyces cerevisiae*—derived from beer-making. When you buy yeast, it's either alive (fresh yeast or cake yeast) or it's active dry or instant. The latter means it's been made shelf stable using a process where living yeast cells are encapsulated with dead yeast cells until water is added to dissolve dead yeast and wake living cells.

All commercial yeast is different than yeast in sourdough. If you were to try to add commercial yeast to sourdough starter, the commercial yeast would die within days. The yeast in sourdough has evolved to survive highly acidic environments.

Sourdough is one hundred to one *Lactobacilli* bacteria to wild yeast. *Lactobacillus* is the bacteria that live on us as humans. It's what's used to ferment food. The bacteria rub off of you onto food and stabilize as a culture, like yogurt. If you have yogurt, you can add that to milk and make more yogurt. If it's a stable colony of bacteria and yeast, that bacteria likely includes *Lactobacilli*. It's lacto-fermented.

Naturally leavened pizza is a lacto-fermented food. That's why it's different from using commercial yeast. When you rely on natural leavening, you make bread most anciently with the least intervention. All you need is wheat, water, and salt.

I've used a starter for dough for ten years, which means I'm *just starting* to figure out how to use it. Levain, sourdough, and natural leavening have been used around the world in different ways. I will outline a narrow usage that works for me to make pizza anywhere. I find naturally leavened dough to be more durable, which is handy when I plan on making dough in a place, country, or climate I've never visited. But again, I use sourdough starter because it *tastes better*.

If you mix commercial yeast and starter, you get the flavor benefits of sourdough and the reliability of commercial yeast. I call it a hybrid dough.

Cloning a Starter

The easiest way to begin using a starter is to take a piece of someone else's and feed it. A glass jar or a plastic container and a scale are all you need. I recommend feeding one part starter with one part flour and one part water. King Arthur all-purpose flour is great because it's inexpensive, widely available, and malted. That malted barley provides yeast a little extra food and makes things more foolproof.

> 50 grams of starter
> 50 grams of flour
> 50 grams of water

Starter Math

If your friend gives you 50 grams of starter from her bakery, take it home and mix it with 50 grams of flour and 50 grams of water. If you want to keep the same amount of starter, discard any extra after weighing out the 50 grams or however much you want to use. For example, if your starter is 150 grams and you want to keep it at 150 grams, weigh out 50 grams of starter, then discard or bake with the rest. Once you mix it with 50 grams of flour and 50 grams of water, you'll have 150 grams of starter again.

Mix the starter, flour, and water vigorously in a container. You now have 150 grams of starter!

You just fed it, so it's not just flour, water, and starter, it *is* starter. It's eating. Now you need to let the colony activate—eat and reproduce. The starter will rise within 2 to 4 hours at room temperature (72°F to 74°F/22°C to 23°C).

Within 4 to 5 hours the starter should almost reach peak size, the height it will reach before it stops growing. Eventually, gas escapes, it collapses, and turns into a mixture that's more of a liquid.

Feed the starter once more the same day. If you want to keep it the same size, remove all but 50 grams of the starter, add 50 grams of flour and 50 grams of water, mix vigorously, and cover. I recommend taking that removed starter, labeling it with the weight and date, and keeping it as a backup in the fridge.

After the first day, feed it twice daily if you want to use it at any time. Just keep it alive and you'll be good.

COMMERCIAL YEAST

A lot of what you'll read about using commercial yeast to leaven bread follows old tropes more than modern scientific understanding of bread baking. I've never found the need to "bloom" yeast, or "feed" it sugar. Salt in your initial mix doesn't kill yeast. It's more resilient than you think.

Fresh yeast (aka cake yeast) is the preferred commercial yeast. If a reliable source for fresh yeast is available, this should be your go-to for recipes calling for commercial yeast. If reliability is important (say you're doing a pop-up in a new city and need to make five hundred pizzas in two days) and a source of fresh yeast is questionable, use instant.

Instant yeast is dried more gently than active dry yeast. It contains fewer dead cells and more usable cells. I try to use minimally processed products of the highest quality. This applies to commercial yeast too.

Active dry yeast is subjected to high temperatures, so most cells are dead. It's a ghost ship of yeast cells. Hard pass on active dry.

Starter Scent Stages

It's important to familiarize yourself with the stages of your starter through smell.

Stage One: When your starter has been freshly fed, it should smell like wet flour. Basically not much.

Stage Two: After three or four hours, you'll see bubbles. You should be able to smell yeasty, floral notes. Nothing will smell sour at this stage. That comes later. This is the stage when I prefer to use my starter.

Stage Three: After anywhere from twelve to twenty-four hours, if you remove the lid and smell your starter, you'll get a burst of carbon dioxide, like opening a carbonated beverage. It will have a boozy, beer-ish, sour smell, which means it has run out of food and stopped reproducing. That's what a healthy starter smells like.

How Long Will It Last?
And How to Bring It Back

A starter you store in the fridge will be good for up to a month before it needs refreshing. It's like having a backup of your hard drive. To refresh a starter, pour off any liquid and feed it using that same ratio: one part starter, one part water, one part flour. Then leave it at room temperature for *at least* a day. After the second feeding that day, it should bounce back. You can experiment by adding different flours, like rye, to whatever you're removing during a feeding. Also try different hydrations, dryer or wetter, and see how the starter performs. It's great to have a backup in case you don't love how an experiment goes.

Measuring Temperatures and Keeping Track

Tracking everything you do with your starter is important if you want to make changes to it or understand its development and what you've done successfully and unsuccessfully. You can't control something you haven't measured. I suggest to clients to take the temperature of their flour and water.

Both flour and starter should be room temperature (72°F to 74°F/22°C to 23°C). Water should be 68°F to 70°F (20°C to 21°C). Because friction and reproducing bacteria add heat, water temperature should be lower than target temperature, the low 70s—a nice average starting point. But remember, sometimes you can't control the temperature of the environment your starter will be in.

You can keep a healthy starter (active and alive) anywhere from 65°F to 85°F (18°C to 29°C). The temperature it exists at will impart different qualities to the starter and different challenges. At the top of the spectrum, toward 85°F (29°C), things move quickly. It will go from active and alive to a dead puddle faster. It also can mean less sour flavor.

You can adjust things based on water temperature. You can control that. If ambient temperature is hot, use colder water.

For instance, I've done testing with clients in kitchens where there's no heat. This happened one winter in Spain, but it's only cold there a short time, so everyone deals with it. They just wear coats inside. We were in this test kitchen and I was wearing a puffy coat (I'm a wimp) and I was freaking out because I had to account for all of this. So the water I fed the starter was warmer than normal.

Dough and starter will move slower in a colder room. If you want to speed things along, raise the temperature. One way to do that is with water. Same thing in a hot environment. If you make dough in a hot, humid place, use cooler water. This shouldn't kill the yeast unless it's in the 40s or 50s, low water temperatures that will shock the yeast.

All you need to make starter from scratch is freshly milled whole grains and decent water with low to no chlorine. If you have a mill, using it is the best way to do it because you're going to see the most activity out of that super fresh flour. Also, it's just cool. It takes less than two weeks, and you'll need some sort of incubator for the best results.

I've found that 78°F to 80°F (26°C to 26°C) is the best temperature to create a new starter. Once you have a stable colony or starter, it's more durable, but when you're creating one, you need to be specific. There are proofing boxes or proofers that help control that range, and a dehydrator is great for controlling temperature. But you can also use a simple insulated cardboard box. I've used a box wrapped in blankets or covered with heavy-duty foil. Put it next to your baseboard heater in your house or another warm spot.

When making natural wine, everything you need to make wine is on the skin of the grape. It's the same with sourdough starter—everything needed to make bread rise lives on the outside of a wheat berry. The grains should be organic and fresh for the best results.

DAY ONE
Start with freshly milled whole wheat, feed it one and a half parts water to one part flour, and put it in a glass container covered loosely. It will be wetter than when feeding an established starter, which makes sense—there's no wet starter component yet. For now, it's just flour and water. Leave it in your proofing box, dehydrator, or wrapped cardboard box for 24 hours. If you've used freshly milled grains, you'll see bubbles after

24 hours. After that, the mixture will smell like wet flour. That will change. Prepare to smell weird stuff.

DAYS TWO TO FOUR
For the first few days, the point is to keep the mixture wet while loosely covered. Feed it once daily for three days with a wetter ratio than normal. For example, 50 grams of starter mixed with 25 grams of flour and 50 grams of water (a total of 125 grams). After four days, the smell will creep in. The smell depends on the wheat used. Mine started smelling like a sweet corn cake.

DAY FIVE
This is the dark time. You want to start feeding your starter a ratio of one part starter, one part flour, and one part water. Things can get weird in the smells department.

DAYS SIX TO EIGHT
Keep this up for three more days. In this dark time, the mixture can smell really off because of a bacterium called *Clostridium perfringens*. From what I've read, this makes sense because *Clostridium* is the bacteria living in your gut.

So, yeah. But it's on you, me—on all of us. So it makes sense it would make its way into this experiment. But it won't survive if you give the right tools to the good guys, *Lactobacilli* and wild yeast. The smells will tell you who's winning. It's a way of seeing, on a microscopic level, what kind of bacteria is in there.

There will be weird ones. The smells can be bad, possibly nauseating. But hopefully, it will change to something that smells like blue cheese (created by another bacteria that lives on humans). We ferment food by transferring human bacteria to our foods and inoculating them.

DAYS NINE TO TEN

It's a free-for-all at this point, and we want it to settle into a stable colony. Keep pushing. Eventually it will smell like Gorgonzola, then Parmigiano, and from there, hopefully, you break through after dark times.

DAY ELEVEN

Start feeding it with the one-to-one-to-one ratio twice daily. That will power us through this last stage to a stable colony. Keep smelling. Once it mellows—when you smell bready, yeasty, nutty smells—you're close. Switch to feeding with white flour—a good unbleached unbromated, organic, all-purpose flour.

Once your starter has that good yeasty bread smell, it can be removed from the proofing box and fed twice a day (one to one to one) and left at room temperature. You're ready to make pizza! You can put it in the refrigerator and go into a two-week feed-and-refresh schedule to make life easier when you aren't making pizza.

I've ordered starters online, borrowed them from people, and made them myself. When asked the benefit of using a starter I created, I'm honest. Bragging rights, understanding the process, and a connection with the wheat you wouldn't otherwise have.

If you don't have a sourdough starter you can substitute with a commercial yeast pre-ferment, aka biga, sponge, or poolish. Here is a recipe that you can use anywhere sourdough is called for.

Pre-ferment instructions
(aka biga, sponge, poolish)

70 grams (6 tablespoons) water

0.5 gram (¼ teaspoon) instant yeast

80 grams (½ cup) high-protein
or bread flour

In a bowl put room temperature water and instant yeast, and mix together until dissolved. Add flour and mix vigorously until it completely comes together. Cover the bowl and allow it to sit at room temperature for 3 to 15 hours (it should double in size) before using it as a substitute for sourdough starter to make pizza dough.

Acidity, Pineapple Juice, and Your Starter

Some people swear by adding acidity. The theory is sound—the idea that you're supporting good guys by putting the bad guys (who can't live in a highly acidic environment) at a disadvantage. So for example, if you add acidity in the form of pineapple juice, it will help create an acidic environment. I haven't tried this, but it works without pineapple juice, so why add an extra ingredient? In eastern Turkey when wheat was first harvested, they didn't have pineapples and made it happen. Skip the juice.

OVENS

WOOD FIRE

Cooking with wood fire is what hooked me on making pizza professionally. It changed my life. Since my early days parked in front of a wood-fired pizza oven for hours, I've traveled around the world and cooked thousands of pizzas in gas deck ovens, electric Neapolitan-style ovens, home electric ovens, and rotating gas ovens. Imagine the oven, chances are I've cooked pizzas in it.

But if I had to pick *one* way to cook pizza the rest of my life it would be wood fire.

Wood ovens are made differently around the world. Not surprising considering it's the most ancient way of cooking. The majority of human meals over history have been cooked with a wood fire or hearth.

Today there are two main types of Italian-style wood-burning ovens: masonry and modular.

MASONRY PIZZA OVENS

The more ancient way. Masonry ovens are built in the shape of a dome with an opening and a flue to vent smoke. They employ fire bricks treated to resist high temperatures. Modern fire bricks (vitrified ceramic that looks and feels like brick) are made with a formula that makes them heat-resistant and poor conductors so they act as a thermal battery that retains heat.

Oven

The Wood

It may seem obvious, but dry wood is important. Wood moisture content should be below 20%. Just-cut trees have a moisture content of 100%. Firewood is cured to achieve the correct moisture level. It should be chopped, which in the industry we refer to as triple-cut—two inches square (although you can use bigger pieces to start the fire). That allows a big flame and control. Feed it with smaller pieces so you get a big flame and it doesn't turn into a pile of coal.

but generally, steady heat means more consistent results. I started making pizza using a Pavesi Forni modular wood oven from Modena, Italy. Maybe if I'd started with a masonry oven I'd be partial to that, but I'm a fan of modular concrete ovens. I love the idea of mixing ancient design with modern techniques. There are also fewer floor pieces, making it easier to clean, with fewer places to snag dough on seams.

I love Pavesi, Acunto Mario, and Stefano Ferrara ovens. Marra Forni and Forno Piombo ovens, which are done in an Italian style but are made in America, are also good.

The Importance of the Andiron

If you don't use an andiron, your fire will rage, but at some point, the flame will die and leave you with embers. You'll put another piece of wood on to cook pizza with. It will catch, but the flame will die again. More embers. You'll keep adding wood because you want that flame and the ember pile will grow. This does two things. First, it creates an ash pile that takes up space. Second, while it generates heat, it's not the right *type* of heat. You won't get the open flame and radiant heat that colors pizza nicely and makes it spring properly. With the andiron, the wood goes from open flame to ash, so no coal buildup—you'll have the same amount of coals all day.

Building and Maintaining a Fire

The thing that made me fall in love with wood-fired cooking is the early morning time spent by myself starting a fire. It's one of my favorite things about being a pizza maker. It gets the blood going, it grounds you, and it connects you to process. In most kitchens, there's a disconnect because of technology—gas comes from a mysterious underground line and your six-burner is this equipment you couldn't make if you wanted. I've assembled wood-fired ovens and spent mornings chopping wood (a great way to start the day). It's romantic, but also practical to have that connection to process. If civilization ends, I'm going into the woods to build a pizza oven. A dream and nightmare!

Here's my philosophy on building the best fire for a wood-burning pizza oven. How you do it, the wood used, wood size, and dryness of the wood are important.

I start, if it hasn't been done (and to be safe anyway if it has), by sweeping out ash and scooping out anything in the oven into a metal fire bucket. Then I put two big squared-off pieces on the bottom of the oven, side by side with an empty channel running from the oven's mouth to the back. I center this stack under the keystone at the apex (the highest point) of the oven roof, then alternate, cross-stacking two medium-sized pieces side by side and perpendicular to the wood below, repeating with smaller pieces, Lincoln Logs style to the top of the dome. Bigger pieces on the bottom, smaller pieces toward the top, with kindling and small pieces and paper on top. If you're starting a fire in an oven used every day, there will be residual heat, so one trick is to close the oven mouth and let your stack preheat and dry. After forty-five minutes you can light a fire from the stack with one match almost immediately.

When a fire is built correctly, the fuel (oxygen rushing in) will shoot up the middle of the stack like a chimney, and at the top, flames will hit the keystone. The faster the fire heats, the less smoke.

Use visual indicators. There will be lots of smoke, the top of the oven will go black, the fire will get so hot there won't be smoke, and the roof will turn white. That color change will creep down the side. When there's a raging fire, no soot, and the oven burns clean, you've reached max temperature.

Move your fire to the side, right or left depending on your kitchen layout. You'll have an andiron on that side to rest wood on above the floor so air flows beneath the wood. Maintain the fire so it burns clean. Temperature will vary. It will be very hot next to the fire and under the dome, and cooler toward the mouth, with the floor around 800°F to 1,000°F (427°C to 538°C).

At night's end, spread your coals evenly across the oven floor and close the mouth.

Wood-Fire Oven Tool Care and Maintenance

All tools should be cleaned and inspected *every day*. A backup of each tool is important, as each tool is essential for pizza production. I use Gi.Metal, an Italian company that's the industry standard for wood-fired oven tools (they make good tools for deck ovens too).

PERFORATED METAL FIRING PIZZA PEEL

A tool for picking raw pizza up (or dragging it onto) from the spot you made it. It's aluminum and perforated, so it stays cooler (less chance of sticking) and allows excess flour to fall through.

The front should be smooth with no dents or snags (they will tear the dough). Smooth any imperfections with a file.

During service, a peel can turn sticky from repeated contact with raw dough. Sprinkle flour on its face and wipe it with a dry rag.

At the end of service, both sides of the head and handle should be scrubbed with soap and water, then drip- or air-dried.

TURNING PEEL

What you use to work pizzas in the oven—to spin them for even heating, to lift and check the bottom, raise pies to the dome for extra blistering or heat, and remove them from the oven. It has a plastic handle at the back and one that slides up and down the metal shaft in front, with a small, flat, round head on the end. This tool gets a lot of oven time, and that front handle slides so you can move up and down the tool without the oven end getting too hot.

This tool can get soiled quickly. It also gets hot constantly so food burns onto it.

The second *anything* sticks to your peel, clean it with a bench scraper. DO NOT wet the peel while it's hot. It will warp the tool! Wait till it cools to clean it.

At the end of service, this tool should be cleaned with an abrasive scrub using soap and water. It should shine throughout its lifetime.

Always use the handle.

OVEN BRUSH

Used to sweep the oven clean of ash and food residue. The brush should be rotated daily or bristles will warp in one direction and it will need replacing every six months.

Brass, copper, or steel bristles only (fiber will catch fire), and since the head is wood, don't sweep for too long at one time in a hot oven.

ASH SCOOP

A shovel-looking thing at the end of a long handle that allows you to scoop ash out so you can bake with a clean oven (its edges are good for getting ash from the oven corners).

This tool only needs replacing if the scoop snaps from the handle.

ANDIRON

Important and often overlooked, this tool provides a resting place for wood so air flows under the fire, preventing a large coal pile.

After a year the horizontal bar will warp. Replace it. A warped andiron won't allow proper airflow.

GAS AND ELECTRIC PRO OVENS

Gas is good for getting started, but the way it moves around the oven can be temperamental. If you can't use wood, go with electric. Electric ovens perform great, are more energy-efficient, and are more environmentally friendly than gas.

ELECTRIC OVENS

I love PizzaMaster Electric Pizza Ovens. They've pretty much taken over New York City's up-and-coming pizza scene. Izzo Forni and Moretti make high-temperature, more open mouth, Neapolitan-style electric ovens that are great. More and different electric ovens will come out—this is the future of pizza. There are places doing amazing things with them. I've worked with them all over the world.

Oven

HOME OVENS

My earliest pizza memories are of pies cooked in a home oven. Specifically, in Grandma Mary and Grandpa Tony's house in Marlin, Texas, about forty-five minutes southeast of Waco, and cooked by Great-Grandmother Lena during big family gatherings.

Great-Grandma Lena's house was next door to my grandparents' house. She had a big garden in between, and she made square pizzas heavy on the home-grown tomato but never featuring mozzarella. Lots of sauce, breadcrumbs, olive oil, onions, green olives, and very little cheese—only Pecorino and Parmigiano. My father's family was part of a community of Sicilian farmers along the Brazos River Valley. Sometimes relatives brought products from Houston, where the Italian immigrant community was stronger, but our access to Italian products *not* grown in the garden was limited to Progresso, a company founded in 1942 by Sicilian immigrants in New Orleans.

Grandma pizza was served as a side with veggies and pasta. It was my favorite thing at these gatherings. The other major childhood pizza memory was a place called Nick's Great Pizza way outside Austin on a road called 2222. Nick (I assume he was Nick) was an old guy from the East Coast who wore glasses taped at the nosepiece and who sported a tank top and white apron. He made cracker crust pies judiciously topped with cheese and tomato finished with tons of Parmesan (definitely not Parmigiano-Reggiano). And then there was Pizza Hut, which was actually good

These three styles form the foundation of my pizza memory. These are my baselines. I don't know how to recreate Nick's, but I can show you how to make the other two (see page 116 and page 136).

I won't lie and say you can make great Neapolitan pizza in a home oven, unless your home oven is a wood-fired oven. But I can show you how to make great pies.

The thing to remember is that an oven has one job in pizza making: Get as hot as it can. With pizza, it's near impossible to get your oven too hot. I've cooked thousands of pizzas and I'd say 90 percent were in a wood oven over 800°F (427°C) and often almost 1,000°F (538°C) on the oven floor.

A home oven without modifications won't get close to that. We're going to shoot for 475°F (232°C) or higher. I've been in situations the world over making pizza in unfamiliar pizza kitchens for pop-ups, unfamiliar non-pizza kitchens, friends' homes, and unfriendly homes, and I've discovered some tricks and hacks.

I learned to always have a backup plan, especially if you're making more than two pizzas. I want you to be confident you can make it work at home—you just have to know what you're working with and have a plan.

How to Trick Out Your Oven

The important thing is having thermal batteries (steels and/or stones) above and below. The key is to create a sandwich with the pizza in the middle. The battery on the top needs to be wider than the one on the bottom, allowing the heat to rise and get trapped between the two, creating a hot zone between them: an oven *within* an oven. You'll get close to a high-temp pizza oven, maybe even a coal oven.

For my home setup I use a wide custom baking steel on the top oven rack and a 13-inch (33-cm) square baking steel on the bottom rack. Stones go on the bottom steel and the pizza goes directly on the stones. It gets *hot*.

If you're *really* serious, you could lean tiles against the oven's *sides* too (just don't go crazy trying to line them up). This creates an area about 100°F (38°C) hotter (you can do this for $100 or less at your local hardware store).

THERMAL BATTERY

THERMAL BATTERY

Home pizza making has been transformed in the last few years, and it's due to high-temperature pizza ovens for home cooks.

Dough Weight for Breville's Smart Oven Pizzaiolo

For the best results with the Neapolitanish doughs we'll be using, I recommend Breville. As far as the size of your dough balls, from 180 to 230 grams. And yes, use a digital scale! A 230-gram round will get a little big for the oven because you want room around the edges for even color.

You've got your Roccbox, a portable, insulated, wood- or gas-fired stone floor oven and your Ooni, a portable pellet oven. If you have a backyard, they're great. The deck heat comes from the flame rolling over the top on the underside of the oven roof, so in that way, it's similar to a wood-fired oven. But it can take time to get back to temp if you're making a bunch of pizzas. And they're no good for lower temp–style pizzas. It's difficult to do coal or gas oven style because heat only comes from the top.

The one I use most, that I've tested for this cookbook and that I've made *hundreds* of pizzas in, is the Breville Smart Oven Pizzaiolo. I *get* electric pizza. I've used high-temperature electric pizza ovens professionally for years. Breville's version is a tiny version of the PizzaMaster. What I like is the ability to control heat from the bottom *and* top. You get that with Breville. That gives you the crust blistering and color you can't get in a home oven.

High temperature is key to making pizzas that look and taste good. It doesn't matter if it's wood, gas, or electric—once you're above 750°F/400°C (*really*, when you're between 850°F/454°C to 900°F/482°C), you'll produce pizzas that have *that* look—the crumb structure and taste of high-temperature pizza.

Once Upon a Time, Pizza Hut...

To be clear: I'm not a fan of Pizza Hut today. They went from fresh ingredients and good mozzarella to subpar stuff and a mealy, crumbly cheese and frozen dough.

It wasn't always this way. If you look at their old training videos online, they did things similarly to how I train people as an international pizza consultant—how to see if the dough is proofed, when it has risen to the right height, and how to distribute toppings evenly with balance. Step by step, they made pizza for real.

In the '80s, the outer crust had this amazing buttery greasiness. It was crunchy and fried like a donut, while inside it was fluffy. There was a light, too sweet, juicy sauce that was barely there, some oregano, a funky Parmesan flavor, and a glorious amount of mozzarella. Everything was basically a way to deliver a huge amount of melty, stringy, chewy cheese.

You'd bite in and pull, but this cheese string stretched with you. You'd chew and it just kept filling your mouth. Pizza Hut's pan pizza was one of the most satisfying things ever when I was a kid. Yes, there's nostalgia factor, but it's true.

Occasionally, a pizza reminds me of that feeling. In Buenos Aires, this cash-only spot El Guerrin that's made pizza and empanadas since 1932, makes pizza with an insane amount of mozzarella. Every bite is stringy, and the crust is crispy on the bottom but soft inside. It's not par-baked, so at the area where the sauce, cheese, and dough meet there's undercooked dough (in a good way). The same thing happened at The Pizza Company in Thailand.

Suddenly, I flash back to childhood experiences at Pizza Hut I can never replicate in their restaurants today. I wish I had one of those pizzas right now.

Oven

First and foremost I would like to acknowledge my wife, **REBECCA ROSEN**, who worked so hard on this book; everything is for your glory, I'm very lucky to have you.

I'd like to thank **HOLLY DOLCE** for believing in the book, **SHANNON KELLY**, **DEB WOOD**, **HEESANG LEE**, **MIKE RICHARDS**, **LEDA SCHEINTAUB**, **KATIE GAFFNEY**, **JESSICA FOCHT**, **NATASHA MARTIN**, and the rest of the team at Abrams for helping to push this book forward. To the team who worked on the book, I couldn't have done it without you; **ANNA ALTIERI**, **EVAN SUNG**, **MOLLY TAVOLETTI**, **SCOTT WIENER** and especially **ARTHUR BOVINO** for being the secret sauce to finding my voice.

I'd like to thank my **MOM** for teaching me that hard work is the solution to almost any problem, and to not take shit from anyone. I'd like to thank my **DAD** for encouraging me to travel around the world fearlessly and for teaching me about our Sicilian-Texan-American culture, and that all cultures deserve respect, peace, love, and understanding. I'd like to apologize to both of them for giving up the vegetarian lifestyle they raised me with, and to assure them that all of these recipes can be made vegetarian. I'd like to thank my sisters **MARY** and **ANANDA** for inspiring me with their strength and for always giving their unwavering support. Thank you to **RICK** and **PAULA ROSEN** for always believing in me.

I'd like to thank my best friend, **PETER LITSCHI**, for partnering with me through every step of this pizza journey from Austin, to Toronto, to Palm Springs, and more, running ops and making parties happen . . . allegedly. I'd like to thank **DUSTIN REX** for always being down to make it nice and share your time and knowledge in pursuit of a pizza party. To **MATT CALENDAR** for always having the best goddamn hair in the pizza kitchen. To **CHRISTIAN PETRONI**, love you beb, thanks for all your help and generosity. To **BEN TANSEL** for Tanseling the world. To **ZAK FISHMAN** and **JAMES STARR** for being so generous with your pizza kitchen and for generally being great guys. To **IRFAN ZAIDI** and **BEN WISEMAN** for being the chillest pizza dudes out there. Huge thanks to my good friend **KERRY BLACK** for everything, and I look forward to pizza Valhalla. Thank you **JAY STRELL** for being there with the best feedback and advice.

I'd like to thank all of the cooks and dishwashers, and bakers, and porters, and all the other back of the house worldwide for the work that they do; it's been an honor to work with you all, and I wish I could list every single one of you by name here.

A huge thanks to **DAVID SELMAN** (of the Selman Technique™). Thank you **JOHN ARENA** and **BRIAN SPANGLER** for being my pizza gurus. I would like to recognize the amazing **IVY KNIGHT** for being the first person to invite me to make pizza internationally, allez!

I would also like to thank everyone at Bráz Elettrica for believing in me and making me an International Pizza Consultant, especially **RICARDO GARRIDO**, **EDGARD COSTA**, **BENNY NOVAK**, **SERGIO CAMARGO**, **MARIO GORSKI**, **FERNANDO GRINBERG**, and **DECO LIMA**. I would like to thank **PAUL CHO** for being the Pizza Wizard on the ground every day, and for being my favorite collaborator for new pizza ideas. I'd like to thank **ALI KHAN**, **CALE ARMSTRONG**, **THOMAS GILBERT**, **CRAIG OVENSTONE**, **CURT MARTIN**, and the rest of the crew at GA Pizza; it's always one of my favorite pizza kitchens to work in, and one of the best teams in the business. I'd like to thank **SAM HALL** and **WILL EVANS** for being my collaborators on the **BRICK O MOZZA** at Marquee Pizzeria, something I dream about all the time.

Thank you to **PHIL** and **ANASTASIA** for bringing me to Nashville and for teaching me more about food than I ever taught you about pizza. I'd like to thank **CARLOS NASSAR** and **MARTIN** for bringing me to Bogotá for the very first time to make pizza at Cafe Monstruo, and for my first Lomo al Trapo with Aji Criollo. Thanks **CARLOS LEVY** for bringing me to Panama to make pizza at Barrio Pizza and for my first cup of geisha coffee; bro, you're killing it. Big thanks to **NICK** & **DAN** for bringing me to London to make pizza at Yard Sale; Marmite on pizza, it works. A massive thank you to **ROHIT SACHDEV** for bringing me to Bangkok to share New York–style pizza with one of my favorite cities in the world with Soho Pizza BKK. Big thanks to "**MAX**" **ANUCHA KAEWPHETSUWAN**, **MATTHIEU COLARICCIO**, and everyone else in the kitchen for working with me and pushing the limits of Thai ingredients with New York–style pizza, and for taking me out for Thai food after service. A huge thanks to **DUDA FERRIERA** and **MARCELO PARENTE** for hiring me to help with Lupita Pizzaria, and showing me and Molly around Lisbon; it's really one of the most amazing pizzerias I've ever had the honor to work on, and a big thanks to **PAULO HORTA** for the tour of your amazing flour mill. A special thanks to **NITHIN**, **MUTHU**, **KUMAR**, and the entire Kannan family for bringing me into your home for Diwali, and for making the dream of making pizza in India come true. I'm incredibly thankful to **ABDULLAH AL KHABBAZ** for believing in me, for the pizza tour of a lifetime in Japan, and for putting together a great team; thanks **MARCO** and **DIYA** and the rest of the team. Huge thanks to **ELI** & **OREN HALALI** for bringing me into two really exciting projects, to **NOAM GROSSMAN** for pushing NYC pizza forward with me, and to **GIANCARLO VILLA**, **ROSARIO VIGGIANO**, and the rest of the crews at Upside and Norm's for making it happen every day. I'd like to thank **ANGELES ZEBALLOS** for bringing me to Buenos Aires to work on Atte, truly one of the most beautiful pizzerias in the world, and to **BRUNO**, **RAFI**, **JULIAN**, **MANU**, **DELFI** (Choripan lunch was a highlight of the trip), **GASTON**, and the rest of the team. Also a huge thanks to **ZORRITO** for the great birthday dinner and an amazing Porteño pizza tour. I'd like to thank **BUN** for making me the best marinara pizza I've ever had in Tokyo at Savoy. I'm eternally grateful to **MIWI**, and the crew of Felix, for the incredible tour of CDMX and for hosting one of the best pizza parties ever, and for the tour of **ARCA TIERRA**, truly a life-changing experience. To all the team in Charleston at Uptown Social, thank you **KEITH BENJAMIN** for having the Thin & Crispy vision, to chefs **JONATHAN KALDAS** and **ALEC GROPMAN** for all the hard work and for the ButterCrust pizza parties. To **JOHN** and **JEN HRIVNAK** for bringing me to Altoona and for being so dedicated to the transformative powers of pizza. To **RYAN MCGINLEY** for bringing me to the pizza mecca of Staten Island. To **JULIA** and the team at Joy Hill in Denver, thanks for believing in me and for staying true to your vision. To **GREG SHUFF** and the team at Roebuck in Chicago for bringing me to one of the great pizza cities in the world to help with your project.

To **LUCY MARTYN**, **ALLY BARAJAS**, **JEANETTE FISCHER**, and the rest of the team at Breville for your support and contributions to the pizza community. To my mozz man **ANTHONY GATTO** for all your support. To the pepperoni king himself, **DARREN EZZO**, for all you do for pizza.

Muchas gracias, **PABLO NIETO**, for bringing me to Madrid to make pizza with some of the best ingredients in the world; can't wait to come back. I'd like to thank **JASON LEEDS** and **CHRIS LIEN** for being the bestest pizza bois around. To **ADAM ELZER**, **PERRY**, **JUAN**, and the rest of the Sauce Pizzeria crew for executing one of the best NY slice projects in the city, very proud of the work we do together. To **TONY** and **GUY PIOMBO** for making amazing ovens and bringing me to Napa, one of my favorite places to make pizza in the world. To **ROSS MOLLISON** for throwing great holiday parties, for injecting magic into pizza, and for allowing me to be your I.P.C., and to **MATT HODGES** and the rest of the team at No Pants. To **PETER DEJONG** for all your support over the years. Thanks to **CHRIS** and **ABBY CANNUCCIARI** for all your help.

And finally, to all the farmers, dairy producers, ranchers, butchers, millers, forklift operators, and delivery drivers: you all contribute to the happiness that pizza brings to people around the world. No pizza maker does it alone, especially not me.

Editor: Shannon Kelly

Designer: Heesang Lee

Production Manager: Kathleen Gaffney

Library of Congress Control Number: 2020944158

ISBN: 978-1-4197-4784-7

eISBN: 978-1-64700-290-9

Printed and bound in China

10 9 8 7 6 5 4 3 2 1

The author has worked with BelGioioso Cheese Inc.,
Ezzo Sausage Company, and Breville, whose products are
mentioned in this book, but the author has received no
compensation from these entities for including them.

Abrams books are available at special discounts when
purchased in quantity for premiums and promotions as
well as fundraising or educational use. Special editions
can also be created to specification. For details, contact
specialsales@abramsbooks.com or the address below.

ABRAMS The Art of Books
195 Broadway, New York, NY 10007
abramsbooks.com